T0352572

HISTORIC ROCKY MOUNTAIN NATIONAL PARK

Historic Rocky Mountain National Park

The Stories Behind One of America's Great Treasures

Randi Minetor

LYONS
PRESS

Guilford, Connecticut

An imprint of The Rowman & Littlefield Publishing Group, Inc.
4501 Forbes Blvd., Ste. 200
Lanham, MD 20706
www.rowman.com

Distributed by NATIONAL BOOK NETWORK

British Library Cataloguing in Publication Information available

Library of Congress Cataloging-in-Publication Data
Names: Minetor, Randi, author.
Title: Historic Rocky Mountain National Park : the stories behind one of America's great treasures / Randi Minetor.
Description: Guilford, Connecticut : Lyons Press, [2019] | Includes bibliographical references and index.
Identifiers: LCCN 2019003953 (print) | LCCN 2019004008 (ebook) | ISBN 9781493038770 (e-book) | ISBN 9781493038763 (pbk. : alk. paper)
Subjects: LCSH: Rocky Mountain National Park (Colo.)—History. | Rocky Mountain National Park (Colo.)—Biography.
Classification: LCC F782.R59 (ebook) | LCC F782.R59 M56 2019 (print) | DDC 978.8/69—dc23
LC record available at https://lccn.loc.gov/2019003953

Contents

Acknowledgments

When you're challenged with telling the stories that shaped a national park, it's extraordinarily helpful to have a historian who takes an interest in your work. Many, many thanks to Kelly Cahill, curator at Rocky Mountain National Park, for sending me dozens of scanned documents and files, tracking down photos, and giving me lots of solid leads for the information I sought. This book would not have come together nearly as successfully without her assistance, and I am very grateful for her patience with my inquiries and her responsiveness.

Thanks also to the folks at History Colorado and the Denver Public Library for access to their photo files, and to journalist and historian Kenneth Jessen for pointing me in the right directions for these photo sources. I also thank Norma Platt for the loan of *Grand Lake: The Pioneers*, written by her relative Mary Lyons Cairns.

The staff at Lyons Press has once again come together to create a beautiful book. My editor, Holly Rubino, heads a team that includes production editor Meredith Dias, copy editor Helen Subbio, layout artist Jason Rock, and proofreader Roberta Monaco. I also thank my wonderful agent, Regina Ryan, who has guided my career for thirteen years and continues to make sure I get great assignments and regular paychecks.

To the friends who have been my cheering section for as long as I can remember, here's another shout out for all of your support and your tolerance of my long-winded stories about national park history: Martha and Peter Schermerhorn, Ruth Watson and John King, Ken Horowitz and Rose-Anne Moore, Lisa Jaccoma, Martin Winer, Bruce Barton, and so many others.

And to Nic, my husband and the best traveling companion a girl could want: Thank you for making sure we get where we're supposed to go, get home again, and have everything we need with us for any eventuality. I still don't know what's in the three magic canvas bags in the back of the car, but they seem to hold whatever will get us out of any jam we may ever face. So far, so good—and so many more miles ahead.

INTRODUCTION

WELCOME TO THE OLD WEST.

Old has an enormous meaning in a place where the first people arrived more than ten thousand years ago and the glaciers sculpted the landscape long before that. As an entity, Rocky Mountain National Park is just over a century old, but its origins extend beyond prehistory, back some eighty million years when a series of jolts of the planet's tectonic plates forced one layer of the earth's crust on top of another, until they formed the highest peaks in Colorado. Launched from beneath layers of sedimentary rock—what geologists call the Ancestral Rocky Mountains—these new mountains began to erode as they met with repeated ages of glacial activity as well as the wind and weather of a volatile planet. Perhaps Longs Peak measured 20,000 feet above sea level at one time; now, at 14,259 feet, it's still part of Colorado mountain royalty as the only "fourteener" within the park.

After the last of the glaciers receded about fifteen thousand years ago, and Rocky Mountain's namesakes displayed marvelous formations of granite and gneiss, people began to find their way here in pursuit of some of the largest game ever to frequent these parts: woolly mammoth, mastodon, and others. They left the scarcest of signs that they were ever here at all, but wily archaeologists put together their story notwithstanding the shortage of tangible objects. Later people arrived who would stay as long as they could: Ute and Arapaho, tribal people who lived in the plains and valleys and hunted and gathered in the mountains, eventually learning an agrarian lifestyle when newcomers drove them off their own lands.

It was these new arrivals, European Americans ready to homestead on land acquired by the United States through the Louisiana Purchase, who triggered rapid change throughout the Colorado Rockies. Filing

Longs Peak is visible all over the east side of Rocky Mountain National Park.
MACKENZIE REED, NATIONAL PARK SERVICE

land claims sanctioned by the government, digging mines when hints of precious metals revealed themselves on the surface, and building guest lodging, dude ranches, and boomtowns, they made new homes here that would establish their dominance. In the space of a decade or so, the Colorado Front Range became the hopeful place for people looking to take their lives in a new direction. It also settled into the lawlessness we see in movies, with shootouts, land grabs, feuding ranchers, and conflicts between settlers and those who came before them.

Somehow, in this chaotic environment, a few people developed a greater vision and a higher purpose, and they invited the federal government into their front yards to create Rocky Mountain National Park. To them we owe a debt of gratitude for the transformation that took place here in what had truly been the Wild West. Park officials reclaimed the wilderness, set boundaries, made rules, and preserved this magical place for the generations to come. In turn, towns such as Estes Park and Grand Lake were transformed into tourist destinations, attracting visitors from all over the world to see the treasures this park is sworn to protect.

Bighorn sheep are one of the favorite wildlife sightings in Rocky Mountain National Park. NATIONAL PARK SERVICE

In this book, I've endeavored to tell some of the human stories that led Rocky Mountain down the path from ancient wilderness to protected gem. This book presents tales of the first people to venture into these mountains, those who followed them, and the daring days of homesteaders, prospectors, cowboys, and dudes. It also reveals the stories of those who explored Longs Peak for the first time and of a few who did not live to tell their own tales. The formation of Rocky Mountain National Park may be about bureaucracy and construction, but it is also about the spirit of a handful of individuals who believed that wilderness should be shared in perpetuity, and about their herculean efforts to ensure that this park will be with us in its current form, now and forever.

Welcome to Rocky Mountain National Park, one of the crown jewels in America's national park system. I hope this book serves to deepen your understanding of this remarkable place and to inform your visit with stories of a past rich with cultures, personalities, and a way of life of its own.

The First Inhabitants

During the past summer I had occasion to travel over and along the continental divide . . . I noticed the debris of very ancient works of stone which, considering their location, were very curious and interesting. They comprised a series of low stone walls, and extending along the smooth summit or backbone of the mountain and connecting to elevated rocky points, about a quarter of a mile apart. . . . The course of these walls was generally north and south with frequent dips, spurs and angles, side walls and pens, forming an intricate system.

—J. R. MEAD
KANSAS CITY REVIEW OF SCIENCE AND INDUSTRY, 1881

J. R. MEAD MAY NOT HAVE BEEN THE FIRST PERSON EVER TO VIEW THE archaeological find he described in a paper in 1881, but he appears to be the first to record his discovery for posterity. His exploration of the high country along the Continental Divide took him somewhat south of the area that would become Rocky Mountain National Park—he described his location as "about four miles west from the town of Monarch"—but he noted that he had heard that such stone structures had been found "on the summit of the mountains further north . . . these are the only ones which I observed in my travels. Their origin and purpose may ever remain a mystery."

He wrote a short paper and presented it at the fourteenth annual meeting of the Kansas Academy of Science that November, and his observations landed in a book the following year. In bringing the stone walls and enclosures to light, however, he became a catalyst for what was to come: nearly a century of exploration of the Front Range of the Rocky Mountains to determine who its first inhabitants were and why they would spend considerable time and effort building low walls on high mountains, twelve thousand feet and more above sea level.

A greater understanding would be long in coming. Abner E. Sprague, a frontiersman who made the Estes Park area his home as a young man in 1875, had his own theory about the high country's rock walls. "Only by hearsay is it understood that trails of communication between the Pacific and Atlantic sides of the Continental Divide in this, the Estes park region, were used in the long ago, either by Indians or some other peoples," he wrote in 1930 in a story for the *Estes Park Trail*, the town's newspaper. "In the late '[18]70s I was told of a wall of rock just at timberline on the east face of the mountain, by the finder supposed to be for defense, or in a manner, a fort." The wall stood on the east slope of Flattop Mountain, its discoverer revealed, "from the Timberline spring to the first ridge dividing the north slope from the east slope of the mountain."

Years would pass before Sprague had the opportunity to investigate for himself. "I visited the spot, located the wall, saw it could not have been built for fun or defense, but did not have time to investigate or learn the reason for it being there," he reported after making the trek up the mountain. "For years I have wished to again visit the place and try to settle the question why so much heavy work was done."

Sprague got his wish in the summer of 1930, making his way back to the wall for a more thorough observation of its construction. "I began at the place where the most of the work had been done at the foot of the slope, through a mass of large loose rock," he wrote. "I soon discovered that the large rock had been moved from a space a few feet wide, and not thrown carelessly to each side, but piled all on the north side. In shape a rough wall: then the spaces between the large rock filled with small stones."

This must be a trail, Sprague determined, and he declared, "The riddle was solved." He went about tracing the length of what he believed to be an old route of passage over the mountain, becoming more certain of his deduction with each sign he found. "The rock that was moved was all

Evidence of Paleoindian activity was discovered at the top of Flattop Mountain (right). NATIONAL PARK SERVICE

to the right as you ascend the mountain," he said. "In places there is a pile of rock on each side, still standing, to guide the travel. This I found to be the case on the ridge, which was as far as I tried to trace this old trail." When he reached the old spring, he observed that a new trail created by decades of recent foot traffic had erased the remains of the old one.

"Who made the trail, and why?" he wondered at the end of his article. "I hope someone will try to trace this old highway from the foot of the mountain to the top and beyond. If it could be traced through heavy timber some estimate of its age might be guessed at."

He did not need to wait long. Dorr Graves Yeager, chief naturalist for Rocky Mountain National Park, soon deduced that this rock wall and others like it throughout the region served not necessarily as trail but as game drive routes, a method the earliest human beings used to funnel herds of large animals along a specific path. Concentrating the numbers of deer, bison, elk, or mammoths through a narrow corridor gave hunters the best opportunity to kill many animals at once, collecting the meat they needed to sustain an extended family unit or a band through a Colorado winter.

Large, dry-laid stone circles along these paths marked the locations of dugout pits—refilled with gravel and dirt over the ensuing millennia—

where early hunters lay in wait to strike their game with spears as the animals passed.

In 1935, archaeologist Elizabeth Yelm conducted a survey of the Flattop Mountain site and became the first professional archaeologist to formally identify its game drive features. In her master's thesis, she described the site as "a series of rock walled blinds, cairn lines, and a 600 foot long, 2–3 ft high, east-west wall," as archaeologist Robert H. Brunswig, PhD, quoted in an extensive report in 2005. She also unearthed "arrowheads, manos, pottery and two Yuma-like [Late Paleoindian-Cody Complex] points," some of which she collected for further study. The pieces have since been identified as the prehistoric Apache and Ute ceramic types from the Early Ceramic Period, from about AD 1 to 1100, indicating that the early ancestors of these tribes used the high country as well.

ARROW POINTS AND OTHER TREASURES

Before Yeager's time, amateur archaeologists living along the Front Range happily helped themselves to arrowheads, spearheads, pottery shards, and other artifacts they found in the mountains, bringing them home to study and display as part of what became vast personal collections. Removal of artifacts from the places they were found, however, reduced their ability to tell the story of their original uses. On a bookshelf or in a glass case, the physical context in which these items were found, the other artifacts that may have surrounded them beneath layers of dirt and gravel, and their role in the greater picture of prehistoric life in Colorado became lost to history. Yeager stepped into this collecting culture and began to change it, advocating for the study of artifacts in situ and gaining all the insights possible from their location and surroundings before gathering them and placing them in museum cases.

Now these items could tell a more complete tale. Archaeologists started to make exploratory trips to Colorado's mountain ranges in 1932, led by the Colorado Museum of Natural History, the University of Colorado, and the Smithsonian Institution, to dig into the pits and along the walls. For the first several decades of their interest, they focused on areas to the south and east of the Rocky Mountains, leaving the secrets of the national park for another time. These explorers of the continent's past had a hand in determining the whereabouts of the first human beings to inhabit what would become North America, why they were there, and what their lives may have been like.

Piecing together a history based on bits of chipped stone, lumps of ancient charcoal, and splinters of broken pottery requires expertise that goes far beyond one team's conjecture. These academically trained professionals drew on the knowledge of researchers from as distant a place as the Bering Strait in northern Alaska, connecting the dots between discoveries farther north and west to build a framework—albeit a murky one—of the lives of the first people to set foot on these high mountain passes thousands of years ago.

Archaeologists have worked for decades to understand how Paleoindians used the area above the treeline. NATIONAL PARK SERVICE

During the last days of the Ice Age (or Pleistocene Age), glacial ice sheets that had covered most of Europe, North and South America, and some areas of Asia over the preceding 2.5 million years finally began to recede. From under the ice emerged a land bridge between far northeastern Asia and northwesternmost Alaska. Nomadic hunters, people who had evolved in the warmer African and Asian climates, had migrated north through Asia and now crossed over from one continent to the other in pursuit of big game, which very likely preceded them on this route. As ice melted and the planet warmed, they eventually made their way down through Canada and into the plains west of the Rocky Mountains, a journey that probably took many decades.

As written language did not yet exist, we have no historical records to tell us how these people lived or what kind of culture they may have shared. Scientists have used the relics left behind to understand when these people were here, what use they might have made of the natural resources around them, and why they chose the land above the tree line for their big-game hunting.

Radiocarbon dating of charcoal and pottery shards, a capability gained in the 1940s, placed the artifacts found in Rocky Mountain National Park in about 10,000 BC. Here the earliest human visitors encountered high-altitude lands covered in ice and persistent glaciers among the high peaks—an area not suitable for building year-round camps but quite attractive for hunting the large animals that sustained them. At the Dent archaeological site a few miles east of the park, in fact, archaeologists in 1960 discovered—alongside Clovis points, the oldest of the stone projectile points found in the United States, dating back to 11,500 BC—the remains of a dozen mammoths. Those who excavated this site surmised that the first people in this area hunted these now-extinct animals as far back as twelve thousand years ago.

Archaeologists named these people Paleoindians and began to draw conclusions about the ways they used the structures they left behind atop Flattop Mountain and other summits in the park. In addition to the Clovis points, they found Folsom points within the boundaries of the park along Trail Ridge, which they attributed to weapon and toolmaking from 9500 to 8000 BC.

The earliest people in this region encountered persistent glaciers remaining from the last Ice Age. LIBRARY OF CONGRESS

A young archaeologist named Wilfred M. Husted, completing his master's thesis on the park's first inhabitants at the University of Colorado in 1962, surveyed the area again and found more than thirty points from the Early Archaic period, placing them in an era between ten thousand and three thousand years ago. Based on these discoveries and others, he surmised that Paleoindians may have made use of the park's high country as far back as fifteen thousand years ago. In the spirited language of the young discoverer, he declared that the high country within the park held "little interest for peoples adapted to hunting the mammoth and the bison."

James Benedict disagreed. Trained in geology at the University of Wisconsin, where he earned a PhD, Benedict spent his forty-year career conducting archaeological excavations in northern Colorado. He made his first major expedition to the high elevations of the Colorado Front Range in 1969, exploring the area at Rollins Pass near Mount Epworth in Rocky Mountain National Park. The more Benedict and his cohorts found here, the farther it led them into the Front Range. By the time he completed his first progress report to the National Science Foundation on his summer's fieldwork, he had discovered ninety previously unknown sites, sixty-four of which were campsites along the edges of the subalpine forest. "This is the upper limit of wood for fire," he said in his report, drawing the most practical conclusion to date about the location of so many camps. "Water is abundant and reliable. Krummholz spruce and fir trees provide protection from the wind and eliminate the need for elaborate shelter. Perhaps most important, the ecotone region contains sources of food that are native to both the spruce-fir forest and the alpine tundra." The ecotone region refers to an area at 11,000 to 11,500 feet in elevation, forming a transition from forest to tundra. Benedict found twenty-five of the campsites in this transitional band, more than in any other part of the high country.

"Although we have little information about Paleo-Indian utilization of the high mountain region, it is clear that the crest of the Colorado Front Range—at least for Archaic and later peoples—was more than just a barrier to be crossed," he wrote in his report. "Passes were heavily utilized. Much of their utilization, however, stemmed from the fact that they tended to concentrate animals in places where they could be efficiently hunted. Game-drive systems occur on all five major passes within the survey area, and are common throughout the region above timberline. They are the outstanding archaeological feature of the alpine region."

He drew the one conclusion that he and others who surveyed the area embraced as the most likely theory of early human existence there:

The sizes of many of the systems and their apparent re-use and modification are not consistent with casual hunting by people whose major intent was to cross from one side of the mountains to the

As Taylor Glacier and others succumb to climate change, more evidence of early human activity may emerge. LIBRARY OF CONGRESS

other as quickly as possible. I suspect, instead, that we are dealing with a tradition of seasonal transhumance, with a regular pattern of movement between the foothills of the Front Range and the high mountains along the continental divide. Summers were spent moving north and south along the axis of the range, camping in the high valleys and hunting at first one game-drive system and then another. Winters were spent in rock-shelters and protected open sites at lower elevations.

9

Research and surveys continue today in the park, opening doors to a better understanding of what life may have been like when woolly mammoths and other creatures grazed above the tree line and people sought ways to control and outsmart the animals for their own livelihood.

The Ute and the Arapaho

Sinawav is the Creator of the Ute people. One day he cut sticks and put them in a bag. He gave the bag to Coyote. "Carry this bag over the hills, and into the sacred ground of the valleys. Do not open the bag until you get there."

Coyote, however, was too curious to obey. He opened the bag as soon as he was beyond Sinawav's sight. Once the bag was open, people began to come out of it. Each person spoke a different language. Coyote tried to gather them up and put them back in the bag, but they ran off in many directions. Only a few remained in the bag.

Horrified at what he'd done, Coyote did not open the bag again and continued to the sacred ground. Here he opened the bag and let out the people inside. They became the Ute tribe.

Sinawav became very angry when Coyote told him what he had done. "The people who escaped will always be at war with the Utes," he said. "They will try to take their land. But the Utes will be the strongest and bravest. They will defeat the others. They will keep this land."

—TRADITIONAL UTE CREATION STORY

WHO DESCENDED FROM THE PALEOINDIANS? THERE'S NO DNA EVIdence to tell us for certain, but history and oral tradition have provided some fairly solid leads. The link between the continent's most ancient people and those whose history we can trace back by thousands of years occurs within the range of 5000 to 4000 BC, when structures, stone circles, pits lined with stones, and other artifacts begin to look like those used by tribes in much more recent years.

Archaeologists have determined that such finds within Rocky Mountain National Park are from the Western Archaic period, and they are like those found throughout the mountains as far north as Alberta, Canada, and west all the way to the White Mountains of California. These finds match the distribution of a family of people who spoke Utaztekan, the root language for a number of tribes, including the Ute, Northern and Southern Paiute, Shoshone, and Comanche peoples.

"The logical inference, and probably the best hypothesis at the present time is that the Intermountain West was the homeland of the Proto-Numic and probably the Proto-Utaztekan ancestral community four to five thousand years ago," wrote Clifford H. Duncan, an elder of the Ute Indian tribe of Utah, and James A. Goss, PhD, of Texas Tech University, after a joint consultation in the park in August 2000, "and that much of what archaeologists call the Western Archaic represents material traces of this ancestral culture."

Stories of the Ute people do go back thousands of years, intercepting the lineage of the nomadic people who arrived at the end of the Ice Age. Ancient petroglyphs found throughout Colorado and Utah indicate that the Ute inhabited the area at least two thousand years ago, and probably for much longer. They lived in seven small bands across Colorado and northern Utah, hunting lands designated for each band and moving from one territory to another freely. The bands all shared a common language and culture, so they recognized one another readily and lived peacefully, often extending their hunting into western Kansas and Oklahoma, the Texas panhandle, northern New Mexico, northeastern Arizona, and southern Wyoming.

Ute families moved from one environment to another as the seasons dictated, allowing them to use every aspect of the Colorado landscape for their sustenance. In late fall and winter, they sheltered in the valley, making camp in the canyons as snowstorms and cold weather dominated the land. Spring signaled a move to the foothills to resume hunting and gathering and to prepare for a higher climb to subalpine meadows as summer temperatures arrived. This existence continued for thousands of years, an efficient way of life that made the most of the land, with skills passed down from one generation to the next.

Ute women played a critical role in moving their families with the seasons.
LIBRARY OF CONGRESS

Rocky Mountain National Park contains several sites that appear to be sacred cultural properties of the Ute people. Some are found along the ancient trails used for centuries, while others appear to be placed carefully as "medicine wheels," observatories that overlook reference points on the horizon, from which the Ute tracked the sun's seasonal movements or the phases of the moon. "There is the same meaning and information packed into these 'solar calendars' as we find in the observatories on top of the pyramids of the Mayas, or in the famous Stonehenge of southern England," Duncan and Goss explained. "The ancestors of the Utes in the Colorado Rockies didn't have to build pyramids to put their observatories on high places, they already had the mountains."

It appears that the Ute lived a fairly peaceful existence here for thousands of years with little change in their way of life, until the mid-1500s, when the Spanish conquistadors first set foot in what would become the

Native people migrated to sheltered valleys for the winter, hunting in the mountains during warmer months. LIBRARY OF CONGRESS

southwestern United States. Francisco Vázquez de Coronado led an expedition in search of the Seven Cities of Cibola, reputedly made entirely of gold; but the golden cities turned out to be mythical, and he returned to Mexico City in 1542, virtually penniless and much the worse for wear. While he never entered the area that is now Colorado, he introduced the native peoples across the Southwest to horses, and news of these animals and their usefulness soon reached the Ute people farther north.

Horses changed the lives of native people across the region. The ability to travel faster and farther than ever before allowed the Ute to expand their territories. It was much easier to infiltrate buffalo herds on horseback, so they added hunting buffalo, along with deer and elk, to their options for acquiring resources like hides and meat. They also could travel farther to trade with other tribes, offering buffalo hides, robes, and meat to people beyond their usual territory, to the west and south. In return, they received more horses; foods, including corn and sugar; tobacco; woven items; and guns.

Sometime around the 1840s or 1850s, bands of Arapaho—who also had discovered the benefits of horses—began to arrive on the western plains in a migration from northern Minnesota, and they hunted buffalo in the mountains, sometimes clashing with the resident Ute bands. The Arapahos' imprint on these lands, and their continued presence here once white settlers arrived, led the people involved in making the case for Rocky Mountain National Park to consult with them about their tribe's connection with this place.

"For the park planners, the late-comers, the Arapahos, became the Indians of the Park," wrote Duncan and Goss. "Arapahos were even brought into the park in 1914 to help in naming the geographical features, and the Utes were not consulted. It should be kept in mind that the Utes and the Arapahos are completely different peoples speaking languages that belong to completely different language families."

UNDERSTANDING THE ARAPAHO

There was nothing but water as far as man could see. A man walked around on the water for four days and nights carrying a Flat Pipe. He

The Ute used all parts of the animals they hunted, including the skin of elks to make tipis. LIBRARY OF CONGRESS

wanted to protect the pipe but could see no way to do so. He walked, fasted, and wept for six days.

On the seventh day, he decided that what the Flat Pipe needed was earth. He called to the four directions for someone to come to help find land. He called seven cottonwood trees and animals of the air and sea. Turtle said that land was at the bottom of the ocean, so the man asked the animals to dive down to find it. Many animals tried and failed: waterfowl, otters, beavers, coots, garter snakes, black snakes, ducks, geese, cranes. No one found earth.

Then Turtle dove, but before he did, the man made a ritual gesture with the Flat Pipe four times and then touched it to his body. It turned into a redheaded duck, and he and the duck dove with Turtle. Turtle seized a clod of earth and brought it to the surface. The man dried the earth, divided it into four pieces, and cast one in each direction, creating Earth.

—TRADITIONAL ARAPAHO CREATION STORY

In the summer of 1914, while a number of people in and around Estes Park worked to convince the US Congress to create Rocky Mountain National Park, a small expedition formed for a horseback pack trip. Two Colorado Mountain Club members, Harriet Vaille and Edna Hendrie, contacted the Wind River Indian Reservation, in Wyoming, in hopes of finding members of the Arapaho tribe who had lived in the area before white men settled there. They sought people who would remember places where the Arapaho had camped, hunted, held ceremonies, and used these mountains to their advantage as part of their daily lives.

Tribal police helped them identify five or six people who could tell tales of those days, so Vaille and Hendrie invited them to go on the pack trip. The two-week journey would cross the Continental Divide repeatedly, circling through parts of the proposed park where items from the tribe's past—mostly pottery shards and arrow points—had been found by area residents. They hoped that the Arapaho would recall the names of various places in the mountains in their own language, so these names could be added to the narrative they would submit to Congress. These designations would help make the case that the land should be protected by federal means, in order to preserve thousands of years of human history.

Only two of the Arapaho they approached were willing to undertake such a journey. Gun Griswold, who was seventy-three, had been a US judge on the reservation, while sixty-three-year-old Sherman Sage served as chief of police at the time of the expedition. The Arapahos had not been in the park area for nearly fifty years, so Griswold was a young man of just over twenty years old when he last crossed these lands, and Sage had been a boy of about twelve.

Interpreter Tom Crispin accompanied them, as the two men spoke no English. He held the position of official interpreter on the Wind River reservation, making him particularly qualified to accompany the two tribesmen.

Oliver W. Toll assumed a leadership position on the trip, not because he had significant skills as an ethnographer—in fact, he had none—but

Arapaho moved into the Colorado territory sometime in the mid-1800s. LIBRARY OF CONGRESS

because he happened to be Harriet's cousin. The assignment was not such a stretch, however: At twenty-three years old, Oliver had lived in the area that would become the town of Tolland for most of his life, as his father had purchased nearly a thousand acres of property there. He had often explored the trails and passes of the Colorado Front Range with his three brothers, but he would not have to rely on his own ability to maintain his bearings; instead, Shep Husted, a well-known and experienced guide, assumed the responsibility of bringing the party through the mountains.

They set out on Tuesday, July 16, stopping at landmarks and wide vistas along the way, with Toll asking Crispin, "What do they remember about this place?" Crispin asked Sage, and Sage asked Griswold, an act of deference to the elder Arapaho. Griswold pondered each question and offered what memories he could of the name his people had given the place and how it earned the name. "The Arapaho language is musical, sometimes spoken in a kind of chant with a hitching sort of rhythm which makes it, in its way, exceptionally beautiful," Toll wrote in *Arapaho Names & Trails: A Report on a 1914 Pack Trip.*

The information came in bits and pieces, but it provided enough to assemble an idea of how these people used the mountainous land between the Northern and Southern Arapaho tribes, with bands spread across the plains of Colorado and Wyoming.

Exactly how and when the Arapaho arrived in the Great Plains may never be known, as there are no written records, but more recent archaeology tells us that the Arapaho, along with the Cheyenne and Sioux, conducted hunting parties into what became the national park by the 1840s and 1850s. Physical evidence, as well as oral history and traditions, points to a time in the 1700s when they lived along tributaries of the Red River in western Minnesota, maintaining an agricultural society and planting corn. "With the merging of the gun and horse frontiers, they moved out onto the plains and followed the buffalo hunting tradition," wrote Duncan and Goss.

They lived in small villages of tipis—conical dwellings made of buffalo hides, supported by a wooden frame—and built these to come apart fairly quickly when it was time to follow the herds to ensure their food source. To facilitate this rapid movement, they built sleds that are currently known by their Canadian French name, *travois*, to carry their belongings over the open plains. Before European descendants arrived in the western states, they used dogs, their only domesticated animal, to pull the travois.

Buffalo provided food, clothing, shelter, tools and weapons made from their bones and horns, and even thread to sew clothing and bedding. Every part of the animal had a purpose, leaving nothing to waste; even its hooves were boiled down to make glue. The Arapaho augmented their diet with fish, elk, and mountain sheep, pursuing them on snowshoes during the winter and driving them over cliffs in warmer months. While the men hunted, women gathered all manner of plants, nuts, and berries, cooking what they needed for each day and preserving quantities for winter.

Pottery, a staple of existence for some tribes, did not figure into the Arapaho lifestyle by the time they arrived on the Great Plains. Instead, they made plates and bowls out of rawhide and hollowed-out tree knots, and utensils from animal horns. Woven baskets, rawhide bags, and implements carved from wood served them as well, eliminating the need to create ceramics, an activity closely associated with tribes further south.

When the Arapaho moved through the land that would become Rocky Mountain National Park, they usually did so in pursuit of game, but individuals going alone might choose a place to fast in preparation for a vision quest. "Practically every man made one or more attempts to secure a vision by going to a lonely place, fasting, going without water, praying, and sometimes indulging in self-torture or mutilation by sacrificing a finger joint," wrote Betty Yelm and Ralph L. Beals, PhD, in *Indians of the Park Region*, a booklet created by the park in 1934 to provide detailed information about the Arapaho and Ute tribes to tourists. "If successful he saw in his vision some supernatural being, usually an animal, who became his guardian spirit and endowed him with supernatural power. Usually he was informed that he would be successful in war, would amass much wealth in horses, or become a great doctor. Generally he was taught special songs and instructed in individual ways of dress on certain occasions."

Toll learned where hunting, fasting, and other activities took place in the Front Range, as his traveling companions shared stories they remembered or had heard from their elders. They knew Thatchtop Mountain, for example, as "Buffalo Climb," or *haathaanon-tahou*, as Toll spelled it using the phonetical code he created to record the Arapaho pronunciation. "One winter a herd of buffalo-cows in the Park climbed high on the slope of Thatchtop and were caught there by the snow," Griswold told them. "The Indians climbed the mountain on snowshoes and killed many of them." Steep Mountain had been named "Where the Buffalo Was Chased," or *anáchataanXunant* (the letter *X* is pronounced "ch"), because a group of boys herding their horses near the mountain spotted a buffalo there and chased it some distance up the side of the peak.

What we know today as Old Man Mountain had a similar Arapaho name: "Sitting Man," or *hinántoXthaoXut*, and it became a place where men went to fast and hope for a vision. Buffalo Pass, in the North Park area, also served this purpose, gaining the name "Fasting Butte," or *batásuet*.

Some places got their Arapaho names because of battles fought with members of other tribes. When the Arapaho moved into the area, they essentially invaded territory traditionally held by the Ute, and not surprisingly, the two tribes sometimes clashed. Toll described one battle that Sage and Griswold remembered:

> *A band of Utes were coming up the north fork of the Thompson, when they attacked a few Arapahos, killing one of them, Sage's uncle. The main body of the Arapahos were near by [sic], but for some reason did not wish to attack the Utes directly, so they took a roundabout route into Estes Park, going through the gap from "The Orchard" to the Big Thompson. They fell upon the Utes, who were entering Estes Park on the regular trail from West Creek . . . and drove then back down Devils Gulch, to the park on West Creek below Bullfrog Rock, where the Utes scattered. From that affair this park was known as "Utes Scattered,"* wahtánha-naaXonáthâ.

THE TERRITORIAL SHIFT

In 1848, the United States and Mexico ended the Mexican-American War with the Treaty of Guadalupe Hidalgo, and Mexico ceded its lands north of the current southern border to the United States. This placed much of the Ute homeland under US government. The concept of government in general was a foreign one to Ute and Arapaho alike, so they could not fathom the massive change in their lifestyles that was about to take place.

The US government opened this land to homesteading as quickly as it could put a process in place for land claims by white settlers. Urging people to head west, the United States sought to keep foreign governments such as France, Spain, and Russia from seeing the open land as an easy conquest. Native people across the region found themselves in conflict with wagon trains of settlers come to seek their fortune, claim acreage, and put down roots on land the Utes had used for millennia and that the Arapaho had just begun to consider their own.

Soon the Utes signed the Treaty of Abiquiu, allowing the United States to place military posts on their land and build roads through the territory. The Utes attempted to go on with their lives as before, but they soon found that land they had used every spring and summer for centuries would be occupied by settlers once the Utes had left it behind for the winter. This worsened significantly in 1858, when gold was discovered on Pikes Peak and tens of thousands of fortune-seekers flooded eastern Colorado. Conflicts became inevitable, and attempts to make peace agreements became more and more contentious. A treaty in 1868 fell apart when the United States attempted to take away the Utes' right to land already specified to belong to them; in 1873, the Brunot Agreement fraudulently stripped them of four million acres of land they had been told would remain in their possession.

The Northern Arapaho, meanwhile, signed the Fort Laramie Treaty with the United States in 1851, which guaranteed them the rights to their traditional lands in Colorado as well as in Kansas, Nebraska, and Wyoming, states in which other bands of Arapaho lived. When thousands of settlers arrived in these territories, however, the United States found that they had made an unenforceable agreement. Soon the Arapaho became warriors in the series of conflicts known collectively as the Indian Wars, as the Colorado portion of this engagement found them fighting settlers alongside the Cheyenne.

One of the worst chapters in this ongoing conflict took place at Sand Creek in southwestern Colorado, after a meeting between US officials, including Colonel John Chivington, and representatives from several tribes. The tribal leaders had had enough of fighting; they were ready to make peace and stop living in a constant state of war. At the end of the meeting, Chief Black Kettle believed that a peace agreement had been reached, and he and his people retreated to a camp along the banks of Sand Creek, as US officials had requested that they do. Here several hundred Arapaho and Cheyenne elders, women, and children spent the night with the certainty that their days of fighting were behind them. They raised a white flag of surrender and the American stars and stripes,

An Arapaho in native dress LIBRARY OF CONGRESS

expecting these symbols to signal that they were not hostile, should any troop of soldiers come upon them.

Colonel Chivington, however, had conflicting orders from his superior officer, Samuel Curtis, who told him, "I want no peace till the Indians suffer more." Chivington took it upon himself to make this suffering take place, and quickly. He captured a guide who knew where the camp was, forced him to lead 1,200 American soldiers to it, and as the sun rose on the little camp at Sand Creek, he slaughtered between 250 and 400 unarmed Arapaho and Cheyenne.

It took months for the truth of the matter to come out, but the facts set off a fervor of warfare throughout the region. Chivington expected to be promoted and lauded for his surprise attack, but instead he was removed from his post and condemned by the US Congress.

More than a century later, archaeologists returned to the area to search for remains that would tell them exactly where the slaughter had taken place. Eventually, they found an area with a concentration of hundreds of bullets, Arapaho and Cheyenne artifacts, and the remains of dozens of bodies, indications that they had found the site of the attack. Sand Creek Massacre National Historic Site, managed by the National Park Service (NPS), was signed into law by President George W. Bush in 2005 and commemorates this historic event in perpetuity, telling the story of the atrocities that took place on this land.

Despite decades of resistance and multiple treaties, eventually the Arapaho and the Ute were removed to reservations. Today the Utes live on the Ute Mountain reservation in southwestern Colorado, and on the Uintah-Ouray reservation in Fort Duchesne, Utah. The Arapaho live on a reservation in Oklahoma and, together with the Eastern Shoshone, on the aforementioned Wind River Indian Reservation, in Wyoming.

The Tallest Mountain

On the 30th we left the encampment at our accustomed early hour, and at eight o'clock were cheered by a distant view of the Rocky Mountains. For some time we were unable to decide whether what we saw were mountains, or banks of cumulous clouds skirting the horizon, and glittering in the reflected rays of the sun. It was only by watching the bright parts, and observing that their form and position remained unaltered, that we were able to satisfy ourselves they were indeed mountains. . . . They became visible by detaching themselves from the sky beyond, and not by emerging from beneath the sensible horizon, so that we might have seen them from a greater distance had it not been for the want of transparency in the atmosphere. Our first views of the mountains were indistinct, on account of some smokiness of the atmosphere, but from our encampment, at noon, we had a very distinct and satisfactory prospect of them.

—Dr. Edwin James
Major Stephen Long Expedition, 1820

Meriwether Lewis and William Clark ventured west at the request of President Thomas Jefferson, with the goal of exploring the newly acquired Louisiana Purchase and finding a water route from St. Louis, Missouri, to the Pacific Ocean. They mapped their route carefully and kept meticulous records of everything they experienced along the way, and their journey from 1804 to 1807 became an epic tale that continues to fascinate visitors to the American West . . . but their route took them well north of what would become Colorado, crossing the Dakotas and Montana on their way to the Pacific Northwest.

At much the same time, in 1806 and 1807, another expedition crossed the southwestern territories to bring back information for Jefferson about the Rocky Mountains and the surrounding plains and desert. Zebulon Pike led this courageous trek through land held by Spain, facing capture at the hands of Spanish colonial authorities and transport to Chihuahua, in present-day Mexico, for questioning and imprisonment. Before they spent months in a Mexican jail, however, Pike and his men attempted to climb a high peak in central Colorado, a 14,115-foot summit they decided to try to conquer in November 1806. Sadly, the men had no concept of the challenges posed by waist-deep snow and penetrating cold, and they made it only as far as the smaller Mount Rosa before two days without food, the struggle through drifting snow, woefully inadequate clothing (including a lack of socks), and the icy temperatures forced them to call it quits. Pike named the mountain Highest Peak, but it soon gained the colloquial name Pike's Highest Peak, abbreviated to Pikes Peak through decades of common usage.

Neither of these expeditions passed through any of the land that would become Rocky Mountain National Park. That exploration came after the War of 1812, when the American nation could once again turn its attention and resources to its lands to the west. To penetrate the heart of the Colorado Front Range, President James Monroe and Secretary of War John C. Calhoun imagined a great adventure that became known as the Yellowstone Expedition, bringing together a cadre of scientists, artists, and engineers to explore the mountainous region beyond the Great Plains. Their primary interest was in the booming fur trade and opening a route to the continent's west coast, making it possible to ship furs and other goods from a western port to points across the ocean. To protect the learned men on the rugged route, Calhoun ordered a military complement large enough to intimidate any native peoples who might see the explorers as a target. Colonel Henry Atkinson led the military contingent, while Major Stephen Harriman Long of the US Army Corps of Engineers, a weathered and well-seasoned explorer who had taken on several smaller expeditions

President James Monroe LIBRARY OF CONGRESS

in 1817 to choose locations for military installations, led the scientists and artists.

Unless you are a student of Rocky Mountain history, you may be wondering at this point why you have never heard of the Yellowstone Expedition. There is good reason for this omission from your grade school social studies books: It did not go well. "Unfortunately, the transportation

John C. Calhoun
LIBRARY OF CONGRESS

of men and supplies was undertaken in steamboats, and the experiment encountered many difficulties," wrote historians LeRoy R. and Anne W. Hafen in their introduction to the journal of John R. Bell, official journalist for the expedition that followed, when the journal was published in 1957. "The muddy waters of the Missouri clogged the boilers, and progress was slow. The whole season of 1819 was spent in reaching the Council Bluffs. . . . The ensuing winter spent here was a miserable one, about one hundred men dying of scurvy." The fort at Council Bluffs eventually became known as Fort Atkinson and was located on the Missouri River on the eastern border of present-day Nebraska.

Word spread throughout the country and even across the ocean that the American adventure had met with unexpected challenges. "The

Stephen Harriman Long led the expedition into the Rocky Mountains.
NATIONAL PARK SERVICE

expedition has employed a considerable number of troops, and its objects will not be completed in less than three years," the British newspaper the *Bristol Mercury and Daily Post* reported in February 1820. A man named Ken Herald, identified as "a gentleman attached to the Yellow Stone expedition," wrote a letter to a friend in Pittsburgh, Pennsylvania, as the explorers settled into a wilderness fort in Council Bluffs in November 1819: "The country is a prairie for the distance of several hundred miles back but timbered above and below, which renders it the most beautiful spot I have ever seen for a fort; the scarcity of wood only prevents it from being the first place in the western country. . . . The country is entirely prairie, except a small grove on the bank of the river, but after you get two or three miles back it is all prairie until you arrive near some other water course. I have traveled for twenty or thirty miles without finding a bush of wood or drop of water." He continued, "We have arrived at a very cold climate—it is in the 42nd degree of north latitude, and the immense body of open land makes it three degrees colder. I expect to ascend the Missouri next year, several hundred miles higher, but I do not think the trips will ever reach the Yellow Stone."

This lack of progress led some members of Congress to question the worth of the entire expedition. Secretary Calhoun asked Quartermaster General T. S. Jesup to provide an accounting of the first year of the effort. The quartermaster replied, "On the most liberal estimate, I am convinced that the whole expense of the movement for the present year, including all the supplies furnished by the quarter-master's department, cannot exceed one hundred and sixty-three thousand dollars"—or the equivalent of $3.5 million today.

Struggling with a postwar economy, Congress did not see the worth in this, despite plans to establish a number of additional forts along the expedition's route to protect American fur-trapping interests and shield white settlers from attacks by native people. It voted to slash continued funding.

The public apparently expressed much disappointment in this, because two smaller expeditions still went forward in the spring of 1820. One headed north, opening a route to what became Fort Snelling in southern Minnesota on the banks of the Mississippi River, while the other proceeded west, still led by Major Long.

Long returned to the East over the winter of 1819–20, rejoining the expedition as it moved out of Council Bluffs and made its way to the Rocky Mountains. At the same time, Captain John Bell joined the group. A veteran of the War of 1812, Bell served as commandant of cadets at West Point, a position that brought considerable prestige but little in the way of adventure. When he heard that Major Long had some gaps in his staff of officers, he applied directly to Secretary Calhoun for the post. Calhoun selected him, making him the official journalist of the expedition, and sent him off to New York City to begin his trip west. Bell took a stagecoach across Pennsylvania and boats down the Ohio River and up the Mississippi to St. Louis, Missouri. Then he crossed Missouri and the Great Plains on horseback to join the assembled troops and scientists at Council Bluffs.

What happened next to the men of Long's expedition comes to us through Bell's journal, rediscovered in 1932, as well as through the notes compiled into a narrative by Edwin James, the expedition's botanist and geologist who worked with Long and others to assemble as complete a description of their travels as he could. These two authoritative reports help us understand just what this first group of European-descended Americans experienced as they approached the Rocky Mountains and what their adventure would mean for the future of this spectacular region of the country.

MOUNTAINS IN THE DISTANCE

The expedition of twenty men trekked its way across Nebraska, following the Platte River to maintain its direction west. The men included Long, a topographical engineer and the commanding officer; Lieutenant W. H. Swift, the assistant topographer; Bell; James; a Dr. Thomas Say, serving as a zoologist; Titian Peale, who assisted as a naturalist; Samuel Seymour, a painter sent to capture the landscapes; men named Stephen Julian and David Adams, who between them could interpret in French, native languages, and Spanish; hunters Han Dougherty, Robert Foster, Mord Nowland, Peter Banard, and Charles Myers; baggage master Zachariah Wilson; engagees (fur trappers and traders) James Duncan and James Oakeley; soldiers Joseph Verplank and William Parish, sent to protect the others; and artillery corpsman John Swaney. Later, guide and interpreter Joseph Bijou and farrier and hunter Abraham Ledoux joined their ranks.

"A number of Indians of the Otto nation were present, and remarked that our party was too small, that we would be destroyed by the Indians of the mountains or perish for provisions & water on the prairies," Bell noted in his journal as the group set out from Council Bluffs on June 6, 1820. He also provided a general list of the provisions they carried on six pack horses and mules: 450 pounds of hard biscuit, 150 pounds of parched cornmeal, about 150 pounds of salted pork, "some other small supplies," and five gallons of whiskey. Whether they expected to take water from the river and shoot bison and other game along the way, neither Bell nor James mentioned specifically.

The next few days presented a myriad of hardships. The hunters struggled to find game, restricting the party's diet to the biscuit, cornmeal, and pork in their packs. "The hunters were out last evening but killed nothing, saw a number of antelope that were so wild, they could not approach near to gun shot of them," Bell noted. Rain soaked their packs and provisions, wetting their wool blankets beyond usefulness—and with wet weather came swarms of mosquitoes. Nonetheless, they continued on their route, covering between sixteen and twenty-four miles each day, and reached their first destination, the Pawnee village where Chief Long-hair presided, five days after their journey began. "The village contains about 160 lodges," Bell noted. "To compute the number of inhabitants in this Village, I reckon twenty-five souls to each lodge, which gives me for the whole number of souls, four thousand."

The chief received them with dignity and friendship, Bell said, coming to the expedition's camp and advising them that they might encounter Pawnee war parties along their route, but that the Long expedition should "offer their hands in friendship," and that "it would be well for us to eat with them." The men took this advice to heart and continued on their route the following day, stopping at the Pawnee villages as they passed, reiterating the messages of friendship, and sometimes sharing a meal. At the Pawnee Loups village, Bell noted that the Knife Chief had served to them "too [*sic*] large bowls of corn & buffalo guts boiled . . . in the bowls was spoons for our use made of the buffalo horn—this dish relished well & we eat hertily [*sic*] of it."

The journey continued on June 13, beginning with a crossing of the Platte River, which was "here about four hundred yards wide," Bell said. "We attempted to ride across but the bed of the river being a light sand & in ridges or waves, we were obliged to dismount and lead our horses the water 2 to 4 feet deep—our dismounting into the water afforded subject of laughter to the Indians who had assembled on the bank to see us cross." Once finally on the other side, they made camp not far from the river to "make observations and write the notes, to people to examine their arms & ammunition, to wash their dirty clothes—and in all things to be prepared for a march." Here, also, Bijou and Ledoux became part

This artist's depiction of the Long Expedition captures their arrival in the tablelands at the foot of the Rocky Mountains. LIBRARY OF CONGRESS

of their ranks, joining them early in the morning on June 14 for the long journey across the prairie.

By the end of the following day, the hunters traveling ahead of the rest of the expedition found it virtually impossible to bag the game required to feed the men. Their third day on the march began with the announcement of rationing, limiting each of the men to just one biscuit per day (about half a pound each, Bell noted). "We eat the last morsel of the meat on hand, and a small quantity of bologna sausage manufactored [*sic*] at Pittsburg & brought from there in the Steam boat 'Western Engineer' last year, a composition rather too high seasoned to eat off hand," he recorded in his journal. Long ordered them to make camp early in advance of oncoming rain on the horizon, and the opportunity to remain in one place—albeit while holding their tents down against the wind with their bare hands—allowed the hunters to get them "a fine large buck antelope, on which we feasted in roasted & boiled."

So their days passed, some with meat and some without, some drenched in rain and others steamy with heat, some days devoid of any form of wood with which to build a fire, as the plains stretching in every direction bore very few stands of trees and no forests. As fertile plains gave way to arid, open prairie, however, temperatures became less oppressively hot. "The weather to day has been cool and pleasant, the air, water, face of the country, all indicate our approximation to the mountains," Bell noted, "and in two or three days we shall expect to have a sight of the 'high Peake.'"

The men and their leaders believed that they were heading toward Zebulon Pike's discovery more than a decade earlier, what the earlier explorer had decided must be the highest point in the Rocky Mountains. Little did they know that they would soon behold a higher spire than that one—or that they would be the first European Americans to find it.

More comfortable temperatures and more plentiful meat allowed them to travel faster, covering twenty-two to twenty-seven miles a day instead of the nine to fourteen they had managed in the heat between rainstorms. On Thursday afternoon, June 29, Bell and James both recorded that they could see a planet in the sky. "At three o'clock p.m. the planet Venus was distinctly visible," James wrote. "Its [*sic*] distance from the sun at 3h. 45m. was east 36° 15'. There were a few broken cumulostratose [*sic*] clouds from the south-west, otherwise the sky was clear, and near the zenith, where the star was seen, of a deep and beautiful azure. Our actual elevation, at this time, must have been considerable, and might be supposed to effect, in some degree, the transparency of our atmosphere."

On the morning of June 30, at about 8:00 a.m., the Long expedition had its first glimpse of mountains in the distance. "We discovered a blue stripe, close in with the horizon to the east—which was by some pronounced to be no more than a cloud—by others, to be the Rocky Mountains. The hazey [*sic*] atmosphere soon rendered it obscure—and we were all expectation and doubt until in the afternoon, when the atmosphere changed, and we had a distinct view of the sumit [*sic*] of a range of mountains—which to our great satisfaction and heart felt joy, was declared by the commanding officer to be the range of Rocky Mountains."

Long used his sextant and noted its bearing as S 73° W, and he estimated the distance to the mountain at about sixty miles. Historians believe the actual distance was closer to 100 miles, as the men stood near the mouth of Bijou Creek, roughly near where the town of Fort Morgan stands today. This slight inaccuracy takes nothing away from the moment when Long and his party became the first white explorers to lay eyes on one of the highest mountains in Colorado, at 14,259 feet in elevation, topping Zebulon Pike's "Highest Peak" by 144 feet.

"The whole range had a beautiful and sublime appearance to us, after having been so long confined to the dull uninteresting monotony of prairie country," said Bell.

The men apparently rejoiced in the belief that they had indeed reached the mountain Pike had discovered, and continued to cross the remaining open country, turning somewhat south and keeping the mountains on their right and the prairie expanse on their left.

Five days later, with a celebration of the nation's Independence Day under their belts, the party marched about ten miles and made camp, ready to wait out the rest of the day while Peale and James, accompanied by two soldiers for protection from unexpected hazards, set out to walk into the base of the mountains, "which appeared to be about five miles distant," James noted. They would follow the "Cannon-ball Creek . . . rapid and clear, flowing over a bed paved with rounded masses of granite and gneiss. It is from a supposed resemblance of these masses to cannon balls that the creek has received its name from the French hunters."

Peale and James crossed a plain of "coarse pebbles, gravel, and sand," stepping around a thin covering of prickly pears that seemed to be everywhere they looked. James made plenty of notes about the flora and fauna they passed, from prairie dogs to plants with long quills that stuck them through their clothing. They had walked some eight miles before they stopped, realizing that they seemed no closer to the base of the mountains than they had been when they started. Worse, they had not brought food beyond what they had eaten at the noon hour, leaving them "fatigued and hungry at the distance of eight miles from the encampment of the main body and so far from the mountains, that it was evidently impossible [we] should reach them and return on the same day." They agreed to start back, and by luck, Peale managed to hunt down two game birds—James noted they were curlews—"which were roasted and eaten without loss of time." By the time they arrived at the camp, they had grappled with a number of prickly pears that stabbed their feet right through their moccasins, but they had managed to kill an antelope, a consolation prize for their inability to set foot on a Rocky Mountain.

By July 6, the expedition had lost sight of the high peak they had seen the week before, though they had determined—using some method not detailed in Bell's or James's accounts—that this mountain was not Pike's Highest Peak but a new discovery of another, perhaps taller, summit. Now they could see that the Rocky Mountains were not simply isolated peaks but "parallel ranges, gradually rising one above the other to the centre range of the whole chain." Bell continued, "The first and second have no snow lying on them, they present a rough and broken surface of rock, diversified with a few low cedre [*sic*] bushes—the prairie extends to the base—in some places a short distance up the side of the mountain—as we advance the variety objects along the mountain, change scenery and of views, interest our feeling so much that we forget our fatigues."

Already they had moved southward beyond the boundaries of what, nearly one hundred years later, would become Rocky Mountain National Park. July 7 found them at the mouth of Platte Canyon, near present-day Waterton; by now they were suffering greatly from the unaccustomed elevation, and the learned scientists recommended bloodletting as the treatment for this. Today, of course, we know that the human body requires all the red blood cells it can get to store oxygen until it adjusts to the change in altitude, and that the body will adapt in a few days, but in 1820, reducing blood pressure by opening a vein was considered good medicine. The lack of plant matter in their diet also contributed to their overall malaise, with cornmeal the only vegetable product on their otherwise wild-game-based menu.

So, a few days later, when the party reached the Arkansas River near today's Royal Gorge, they were more than ready to begin the march homeward. "The weather was pleasant, and we was travelling toward home, it is only in absence, that the charms and comforts of home are correctly estimated, reflections brings afresh to our recollection, the thousand kind offices of our friends, which otherwise would never again occurred to us," Bell waxed rapturously about heading east once again.

"The anticipation of again enjoying the benefits & pleasure of civilized society and the fond welcome of our friends, cheers our hearts & gives full scope to fancied imagination in anticipated pleasures perhaps never to be realized."

On July 22, as the expedition prepared to split into two parties—one following the Arkansas River and the other the Red River, before reconnecting in Belle Point, Arkansas, sometime hence—Major Long himself gives us his last impressions of the Rocky Mountains:

The region comprehended within the range commencing on the head waters of the Yellow Stone and extending southwardly to Santa Fee, is made up of ridges of mountains, spurs and valleys. The mountains are generally abrupt, from their bases upward—often towering into peaks covered with perpetual snows, and generally exhibiting crags and knobs, being cut in every direction by deep ravines. The interior ranges and spurs are generally more elevated than the exterior—at least this conclusion is naturally drawn from the circumstance of their being covered with snow, to a great extent below their summits. Altho' the peake which we have denominated James' Peake, is said to be the highest part of the mountains for a great distance around, yet from the circumstance just mentioned, and from its apparent elevation, I should judge, that it is considerably lower than other peaks, particularly, that first observed by us while ascending the Platte on the 30th June. The vallies [sic] are uniformly situated on rivers and creeks, and are many of them extensive, being from 10 to 20 or 30 miles in width. These tracts are generally very beautiful, being rolling or moderately hilly—surrounded by gentle slopes leading up the sides of the mountains, and covered with a luxuriant verdure—they are generally clad with a rich growth of white clover, upon which horses and other animals feed with avidity. The soil is rich, and apparently well adapted to cultivation. The Indians that frequent them, being altogether wandering tribes, and having no fixed places of residence, never cultivated corn or other means of subsistence, to test the qualities of the soil, has yet been afforded. The hills and mountains are generally covered with forest trees and pine near their bases, oak and maple

The first glimpse of what would become Longs Peak must have looked much like this. LIBRARY OF CONGRESS

are sometimes found but not in great perfection or abundance—the growth generally is of a scrubby character.

Long made no attempt to climb the peak that would one day bear his name; nor did anyone else in his expedition. Given the rigors of his journey and the obstacles he overcame to reach the mountains at last, however, he certainly earned the honor of having the tallest peak in Rocky Mountain National Park named for him, a singular commemoration of his achievement in exploration.

The Summit Obtained

*Of that occasion I will say this: never before and never since have I so
completely lost all nerve. I was trembling from head to foot.*

—L. W. Keplinger, 1868

Someone once said, "History is written by the victors," so perhaps we should not be surprised that the history of climbers summiting Longs Peak often omits the local tribesmen and women who may have climbed the mountain regularly, perhaps for hundreds of years. Much of American history seems to begin with the arrival of European-descended explorers simply because no written records exist to tell us the names of the native people who got there first.

John L. J. Hart, a historian writing for the *American Alpine Journal* in 1930, noted, "After the whites occupied the plains and the Indians were driven westward into the mountains, Longs Peak became well known to them. They climbed to its summit in order to trap eagles, desiring their feathers for purposes of adornment." This appears to be well-established fact, as a number of respected historians say the same.

Perhaps they took their knowledge from the words of Gun Griswold, the elder Arapaho who accompanied Oliver Toll on his travels through the park in 1914 to gather Native American names for the park's landmarks. Griswold gave Toll an impressive account of his own father's summits of Longs Peak. "Right up on the top . . . there is a hole dug in an oval shape," Griswold said. "The top of it is big enough for a man to get down through, but it widens out below and is big enough for him to sit in. This was up there when he captured all those eagles, for it was an eagle trap." Old Man Gun sat in this hole, out of sight of the eagles, and put a stuffed coyote and some tallow—rendered animal fat—on the edge of the hole. The eagles saw the coyote and came to get it, and when they landed, Gun grabbed their feet.

The younger Griswold went on to say that he himself had climbed the peak with his father, "from the south side, and had to put on new moccasins every three hours because they wore out so fast. Six of us went up, the rest stayed at the foot. This was fifty-five years ago."

Toll doubted the story because it conflicted with the information he had from William Byers, one of the men in the first party of European descendants to summit Longs Peak (more on this shortly). If it was true, however, Griswold and his family summited the mountain in 1855, well before a company of Caucasian explorers did so in 1868.

So nimble-footed Arapahos—and perhaps Utes as well, though we have no specific stories to confirm this—conquered the mountain long before expeditions arrived from the East, perhaps making the climb seem that much more obtainable by the white men who came later. "When whites finally reached the base of the peak, the idea of climbing it, of course, arose, but the nearest settlement being distant about two days' ride, attempts were very few," Hart told us. "The peak was a puzzle; three sides were explored and they all seemed impossible."

An obscure reference in a newspaper in Golden, Colorado, in 1860 is quoted by Douglas MacDonald in his book, *Longs Peak: The Story of Colorado's Favorite Fourteener*. Apparently, a Mr. Cromer, not otherwise identified, "visited Long's Peak, last week, and scaled the summit, the view from which he describes as grand in the extreme. Four days were required for the journey thither and back." It seems likely that if Mr. Cromer truly was the first to scale the mountain, he might have made more of the achievement and ensured his place in history, but with no other information upon which to draw for clarification, we must simply accept that the squib has the potential to be true.

Far more convincing is a jubilant 1865 account of a summit expedition, captured in a letter printed in the *Daily Rocky Mountain News* in July with a compelling amount of plausible detail. The seven people in the party assembled camping gear and other provisions and took a four-horse team along the St. Vrain River to "the residence of Mr. Estes," spending the night there before heading to the base of West Peak. They camped on a stream along the snow line, hunted for game the following day, and set out before dawn on Saturday, climbing to the tree line in about three hours, "directly north of the great rock which towers so high above its brethren, when we were overtaken by a storm of snow, the most severe we ever experienced," writer J. W. Goss said. "The wind blew with such force that we were driven here and there like feathers in a gale. We took refuge behind a ledge of rocks and waited till the storm subsided somewhat, when we bent our stiffened and benumbed limbs downwards for a milder climate."

After such an ordeal, the party apparently took Sunday off and tried once again on Monday to reach the summit. They "reached within a few hundred feet of the top when we came to an impassable ledge and had to retreat." Determined to succeed, they set out again on Tuesday. "We wound our way along the southwest side, climbing a bank of snow to within a few hundred feet of the top when we had to climb ledges nearly perpendicular, supporting our weight with our hands, but an hour brought us over these when two of the party stood high above other points in the Rocky Mts, waving their hats to their comrades below, who had become discouraged and given up the chase. . . . J. W. Goss and R. J. Woodward were undoubtedly the first to stand upon its top, and we venture the last that will do so for years, though steady heads, iron sinews and unconquerable wills will carry any one up."

The descent posed equally dramatic challenges, Goss noted, with a storm that coated the already treacherous rocks with ice, "rendering the descent much more difficult than the ascent." However, "the view more than repaid the trouble. To the west worlds of mountains could be seen belonging to this chain, and we think the Salt Lake valley, and beyond the snows of the Cascade range. Two of the great parks lay plain in sight while to the east the winding of the little streams to their junction with the Platte, and its snake-like appearance as it unfolds itself, mid bluff and dale presented a picture of loveliness that fell upon the vision like some pleasant dream."

Salt Lake and the Cascades are far too distant to be seen from eastern Colorado, but it is easy to imagine how climbers dazzled by the vista might believe that the view extended for hundreds of miles.

None of these stories rose to fame or withstood the test of time, however; they ended up in dusty boxes in newspaper archives. The summit story that is cemented in the public consciousness details a high-profile, museum-funded expedition in 1868, when summiting famous peaks became an international phenomenon.

THE POWELL EXPEDITION

Two of the highest peaks in the Swiss Alps, across the Atlantic Ocean, saw their first conquests by intrepid climbers in 1867, when mountaineers reached the summit of the Weisshorn and Lyskamm mountains, each more than five hundred feet taller than Longs Peak. American climbers, not to be outdone, craved conquest of a local fourteener: the craggy, serrated Rocky Mountain discovered by Major Stephen Long and his party back in 1820.

So in 1868, one of the West's most tenacious and daring explorers decided it was time to lead a party to the mountain and make the climb to its summit. John Wesley Powell, curator of the natural history museum at Illinois State Normal University, had lost an arm in the Civil War, but the near-mortal injury had not quelled his zeal for adventure and discovery. The year before, in 1867, he had led an expedition of scientists and naturalists into Colorado to bring back thousands of specimens of plants and animals for the museum. One of this party's most impressive achievements was the scaling of Pikes Peak, a mountain already summited by others but never so carefully studied for the advancement of science.

The summer of 1868 brought another Powell expedition, the beginning of the lengthy exploration of the Colorado River for which he is best remembered. He and his wife, Emma, recruited an entirely new team for the journey, young men looking for opportunities to breathe clean mountain air, gain strength on the trail, and have a true adventure in the untamed western territory. Powell needed this carefully chosen corps to bring back all the botanical and animal samples he had promised to a

John Wesley Powell
LIBRARY OF CONGRESS

total of sixty-seven schools and museums, a staggering obligation that nonetheless helped him raise funds to finance the trip.

The expedition hit the road on June 29, 1868, riding the new Union Pacific railroad to Cheyenne, Wyoming, where they purchased horses to take them southward. This task turned out to be an adventure of its own, as the merchants they found had only wild Mexican ponies to sell, "none of them ever having been backed or lassoed," said Lewis Walter Keplinger, topographical engineer with the expedition, in a paper he wrote several decades later for the Kansas State Historical Society's annual publication. All of the horses had to be saddle-broken on the spot before the expedition could ride off on them. "This they did with results not particularly encouraging," Keplinger went on. "Though some of us had been in the army, we had not been in the cavalry. A dun-colored broncho [*sic*] with dark streaks along the back and down its legs fell to me. Those in charge of the herd told me these were 'bad signs,' and subsequent events justified the warning."

Keplinger watched his cohorts as they attempted to ride and were thrown from their horses one after the other. When his turn came, however, his horse remained "motionless as the sphinx" while he saddled him, stroked him, and eventually mounted him. "Then the spur was applied vigorously, accompanied by an imperative command to 'Go 'long.' And then there was a going. Further particulars will be omitted, except to say that I was finally extricated from the resulting heap of man, horse and saddle."

The troublesome start soon gave way to a smoother route, as the party rode to Denver and up to Empire City, where they added to their ranks W. L. Byers, editor of the *Rocky Mountain News*—a man who figures in many stories about adventures in the early days of white settlement in northeastern Colorado. Together the now larger expedition rode to Berthoud Pass, spent several days collecting high-elevation flora and fauna specimens there, and continued into Middle Park, where they first laid eyes on Longs Peak. "Before leaving Illinois it was understood that whatever else we might or might not accomplish, we would ascend the Peak," Keplinger said. "That was something that had never been done, though many attempts had been made. The old mountaineers had fun at our expense. They said nothing could get there that didn't have wings."

They camped at Grand Lake, which was not so much a city or town as "one log cabin occupied by a trapper," according to Keplinger, and a contingent from the expedition determined that they would make the first attempt to climb the peak. Taking their own horses and a pack animal each with food and supplies for ten days, Powell, Byers, Keplinger, Samuel Garman, and local residents Jack Sumner (described as an "old mountaineer") and Ned Farrell set out for Longs Peak to attempt to scale the mountain.

Making camp at Mount McHenry, about three miles from the base of Longs Peak, they corralled the horses and set out early in the day on foot to find a likely route up the target mountain. They attempted to bushwhack their way along various ridges that looked like they must provide some access to Longs Peak, but over and over they found themselves heading in the wrong direction. "After being baffled in various attempts we came to a ridge ascending from the west, which appeared to connect with and lead to the summit," Keplinger said. "We followed this, stringing along for a distance of half a mile. Jack Sumner . . . was in advance; I was next, at a far stone-throw distance. The ridge grew narrower and narrower."

To his surprise, Keplinger caught up with Sumner, who had sat down on the slim ridge. "Hello, Jack, what's the matter?" he asked the visibly shaken man. "He replied, 'By God, I haven't lost any mountain.'" Longs Peak threatened to be Sumner's undoing.

Keplinger shrugged this off. "I told him I had, and without hesitation I walked over the narrow place. It was not to exceed eighteen inches in width, and to have fallen on either side would have changed altitude hundreds of feet, though of course the descent was not perpendicular."

Sumner watched Keplinger cross the knife-edge ridge, and decided that he, too, could brave it. "He did, but he got down and 'cooned' it," Keplinger wrote.

Soon the entire climbing party had made it across the ridge, but before long they came to the end of what they had hoped would be a passable route to the top. From here, the ledge ended; they could see no way up or down. They retraced their steps and started down, making camp on the mountain's south side with plans to begin again early in the morning, but as they stared up at a formation they called the Notch (what we call the Keyhole today), the route resolved before their eyes and they believed they could see a way through. "A place met our eyes, about a third of the way up, which appeared as though it might not be impassable," Keplinger said. It was just 2:00 p.m. on an August afternoon, so light would continue for some time. "I told them that as I was not at all tired, I would go that afternoon in light marching order and reconnoiter. It seemed useless for the entire party to waste its time the next morning if the place on the mountain was impassable."

The Notch, now known as the Keyhole LIBRARY OF CONGRESS

He left all of his gear behind and set out, unencumbered by a pack or scientific implements, and he reached the spot they had seen from the ground in short order. "When I got to the difficult place I found a way around it, but there was another a little farther which seemed doubtful, so I went on and found a way past that also," he said. "Then there was the summit, temptingly near. I was closer than any mortal had ever been before! Wouldn't it be a bully thing to go ahead and get a scoop on the other boys?"

Keplinger continued through the Notch, and for the first time, he saw the wide-open view of Estes Park far below him. He barely paused for a second or two, however, now seeing the peak and focused entirely on reaching it as quickly as he could. As he proceeded to scramble ahead, however, he paused and made the mistake of looking down.

"There, not to exceed ten feet below and away from me, was what seemed to be the eaves of the world's roof," he said. "I looked to my left toward camp, but the still unascended Peak was now between me and that. A lonesome feeling came over me. I started back."

Going down, however, turned out to be even harder than going up. "I proceeded, keeping farther away from those eaves than when I went up, and where the way was more difficult," he continued. "Finally I got where I could let go without slipping over, and dropped a short distance onto an ice formation in the northwest corner of the floor of the Notch. I feel quite sure that ice has not yet melted away. Of that occasion I will say this: never before and never since have I so completely lost all nerve. I was trembling from head to foot."

Keplinger had additional perils to manage before he reached his colleagues at their camp. By now the sun was setting, and wilderness darkness had begun to descend on the mountain, the kind of impenetrable blackness in which it was difficult to see his own hand in front of his face. He managed to pass through the trickiest parts of the route down before he lost the light entirely, but this still left him some distance from camp.

Powell and his cohorts realized that Keplinger must be somewhat delayed, however, and they gathered bundles of dry firewood, sending Sumner up the mountain to build fires along the route, helping the lone climber find his way down. "To see his fires and hear him hallooing were pleasing incidents of the return trip," Keplinger said. He reached camp at about 10:00 p.m., and while the night grew uncomfortably cold and they had to keep their campfire burning all night, he relished the relief of being back with the rest of the party.

The following day, August 23, 1868, all six members of the climbing group followed Keplinger's route up, turning left when they were close to the Notch and continuing on the line most often followed by today's climbers, through the Keyhole from Estes Park. They crossed over the "eaves" that had stymied Keplinger the previous day, and arrived at the summit without further incident. Once arrived, they looked carefully for

The Powell party became the first Caucasians to see the view from Longs Peak summit. NATIONAL PARK SERVICE

any sign that someone had been there before them and found no evidence of human activity. This led them to pause for a moment to build a cairn as a monument and place a baking-powder can there, containing a scrap of paper with all of their names on it.

"As we were about to leave the summit Major Powell took off his hat and made a little talk," said Keplinger. "He said, in substance, that we had now accomplished an undertaking in the material or physical field which had hitherto been deemed impossible, but that there were mountains more formidable in other fields of effort which were before us, and expressed the hope and predicted that what we had that day accomplished was but the augury of yet greater achievements in such other fields."

Powell went on from this accomplishment to explore the Colorado River from one end to the other, becoming the first known person to complete the journey and bring the Grand Canyon to public consciousness. Of the other men on this expedition, we know that Keplinger returned to the Midwest, established a law practice in 1883, and later became a Kansas state representative and a judge in Wyandotte County. Byers returned to his post as editor of the *Rocky Mountain News*. Sumner accompanied Powell on his Colorado River expedition, manning the sextant and keeping the party on course all the way to Yuma, Arizona, where he parted ways with the explorers and met with one challenge after another until he returned to the Rocky Mountains. He spent the next twenty-five years seeking his fortune in mining without much success, and he and his wife raised three sons.

Samuel Garman returned to Illinois State Normal University, completed his studies, and eventually rose to become assistant director of herpetology and ichthyology at Harvard's Museum of Comparative Zoology. He wrote numerous papers on the classification of fish and reptiles. Ned Farrell wrote a short book, *Colorado, The Rocky Mountain Gem As It Is in 1868*, published by the Western News Company, but his further whereabouts have been lost to history.

Summits in Skirts:
The First Women Climbers

It is one of the noblest of mountains, but in one's imagination it grows to be much more than a mountain. It becomes invested with a personality. In its caverns and abysses one comes to fancy that it generates and chains the strong winds, to let them loose in its fury. The thunder becomes its voice, and the lightnings do it homage. Other summits blush under the morning kiss of the sun, and turn pale the next moment; but it detains the first sunlight and holds it round its head for an hour at least, till it pleases to change from rosy red to deep blue; and the sunset, as if spell-bound, lingers latest on its crest. The soft winds which hardly rustle the pine needles down here are raging rudely up there round its motionless summit. The mark of fire is upon it, and though it has passed into a grim repose, it tells of fire and upheaval as truly, though not as eloquently, as the living volcanoes of Hawaii.

—ISABELLA L. BIRD

THE AUGUST 26, 1871, EDITION OF THE *BOULDER COUNTY NEWS* contained a short article on an unusual occurrence atop the area's tallest mountain. "Al Dunbar from Estes Park, last week piloted a party to the summit of Long's Peak, among whom were Misses Alexander and Goss of St. Louis, the first ladies who ever made the ascension," the unnamed editor wrote.

Two years would pass before anything more came to light about these two women, though friends and neighbors undoubtedly heard about their heroic climb. A Mr. Painter, otherwise unidentified, wrote an account of his own climb of the mountain for the *Greeley Sun*, in which he noted that he had taken a close look at four piles of rocks clearly left there by other climbers as monuments to their achievement. One of these monuments contained a scrap of paper with the names of the two women: Addie Alexander and Henrietta Goss.

Painter's story became the subject of an article in the *Rocky Mountain News* as well, with a little more detail about the two women. "Henrietta Goss' name is on the summit," the reporter said, "but she failed to reach the top when only a few hundred feet from the desired goal. Both these women deserve praise for their muscle and their perseverance."

This is the sum total of what is known about Addie Alexander and Henrietta Goss, though it seems plausible that Henrietta was somehow related to the equally obscure J. W. Goss, who appears to have been the first white person to summit Longs Peak in 1865. Without the power of mass communication that we enjoy today, those who were first at a wilderness feat had much less opportunity to tout their own accomplishments—and the need to do so may have carried far less importance. There is no question, however, that Alexander and Goss made their way

Anna Dickinson
LIBRARY OF CONGRESS

up the area's highest mountain several years before the woman who has often been credited as the first female to do so: Anna Dickinson.

At thirty years old in the summer of 1873, Dickinson had already racked up a number of significant accomplishments. Her upbringing in a Quaker home in Philadelphia, Pennsylvania, had made her a passionate abolitionist and advocate for women's rights, and her skill as an orator led her to take a leadership role on a national level. Her speeches on women's rights, the evils of alcohol abuse, ending slavery, and reconstruction brought her to the public consciousness at a young age—by 1861, when she was nineteen, she headlined a speaking tour calling for emancipation of slaves. Soon she became known as one of the cause's most accomplished speakers, and in 1864, she became the first woman called to speak to the US House of Representatives.

With the end of the Civil War, however, Dickinson's very lucrative speaking career had declined, and she had taken to writing, publishing her first novel in 1868. By the time she visited Colorado in the summer of 1873, the wealth from her days as a speaker had dwindled, and she hoped that her daring adventures in the Rocky Mountains would renew interest in her as an author and orator.

She had already completed a trip by mule to the top of Grays Peak at 14,278 feet in the middle of the night to watch the sun rise from the frigid top of the mountain, and she expected it to be her last major trek for the summer of 1873, but a chance meeting changed her mind: She came upon the Hayden survey, a US Geological and Graphical Survey of the Territories led by Ferdinand Vandiveer Hayden and James T. Gardner. The two men and their team intended to take their scientific instruments up Longs Peak the following day and conduct the first official survey of the mountain. They invited Dickinson to join their own quest for the summit of Longs Peak.

Of the Hayden party, she later reflected in her 1879 autobiography, *A Ragged Register of People, Places and Opinions*, she found "a companionship through a few days of men who ought to be immortal if superhuman perseverance and courage are guarantees of immortality."

She waxed eloquent about Hayden, "tall, slender, with soft brown hair and blue eyes—certainly not travelling on his muscle; all nervous intensity and feeling, a perfect enthusiast in his work, eager of face and voice, full of magnetism." Gardner, she said, was "shorter, stouter, with amber eyes and hair like gold, less quick and tense, yet made of the stuff that *takes* and holds on."

Dickinson tells us little about the struggle to the summit, instead capturing the spirit of her daring band and their daunting assignment to survey the wild Colorado lands: "braving rain, snow, sleet, hail, hunger, thirst, exposure, bitter nights, snowy climbs, dangers of death—sometimes a score on a single mountain—for the sake not of a so-called great cause, nor in hot blood, but with still patience and unwearied energy for an abstract science—no more, since the majority cannot work even for fame." She and her new friends sat around a massive campfire and talked well into the night, telling "strange stories of adventures in mountain and gorge, climbs through which a score of times life had been suspended simply on strength of fingers, or nice poise on a hand-ledge thrust out into eternity, wild tales of frontier struggles—intricacies of science, discussions of human life and experience in crowded cities, devotion and enthusiasm and shown in *any* cause—all things, in fact, that touch the brain and soul, the heart and life, of mortals who really *live*, and do not merely exist."

The conversation, apparently, moved Dickinson far more than the actual act of summiting the mountain. In addition to Grays Peak, she had ridden up Mount Elbert, at 14,444 feet the highest mountain in the Rocky Mountains south of the Canadian border. Longs Peak required her to climb on foot, but even this did not warrant detailed coverage in her autobiography.

Luckily, the *Rocky Mountain News* carried what must be editor William Byers's own account of the summit party (although the writer is not identified), as he had been invited to join the Hayden expedition during their time in the area. The expedition rode out from Middle Boulder on September 10 and made its way to Longs Peak via "a very crooked wagon road" through a particularly picturesque area, passing through the nearly abandoned mining town of Ward and on into the mountainous country. Late in the afternoon on September 11, the group they had been expecting arrived: "a party of nine persons from Estes park," including Anna; her brother, John; her friend and former suitor, Ralph Meeker; and

Some summits in the Rockies can be reached on horseback, and Anna Dickinson had visited at least one of these. LIBRARY OF CONGRESS

five others, guided by area resident Griff Evans. "They had missed their way—or at least did not come by the easiest trail—and had been more than six hours in the saddle," Byers noted. The Dickinsons and Meeker joined the Hayden expedition in their camp, while the others camped a short distance away.

The cooks and stockmen rousted everyone at 4:00 a.m., and the group dined on a "marvelous breakfast" before starting for the mountain-top at about 6:00 a.m., "about half on horseback and the others afoot." (Reports indicate that Anna had purchased a pair of trousers in Boulder for this trek, a deed considered scandalous rather than practical.) After a mile and a half of gradual rise, the riders left their horses and the entire party proceeded on foot. "From there on it is rough clambering over huge masses of granite thrown together and heaped up in the greatest disor-der," Byers said. They took the west face up, a different route for Byers, who had summited the peak in 1868 with the Powell expedition. "Up it the climbing is very bad and steep. It is so steep that loose rock is constantly sliding toward the bottom, rendering the footing very insecure." Worse, they encountered four to six inches of "fresh, loose snow" that made the surface even more precarious.

They followed the edge of the gorge that comes down from the peak until they reached its head, turning onto the path that begins about six hundred vertical feet from the top, taking them along a "narrow, uneven shelf. In some places the cliff above overhangs and it is necessary to stoop and crouch close to the wall in passing along."

About five hundred feet from the top, the writer noted, the route joined the one the Powell party took five years earlier, and they followed it to the top. "Some of the party made the entire ascent from cap in considerable [sic] less than three hours," the writer noted. "Miss Dickinson was three and a half hours on the way, or, counting from the upper camping place which is the usual point of departure, just three hours and ten minutes."

Eighteen members of the party stood together on the summit, and the writer speculates that this may have been the largest group to date to reach the apex of the mountain at the same time. The men in the Hayden party busied themselves with their instruments while the others admired the 360-degree view from every possible angle, and Dickinson and the other nonscientists moved downward—"more tiresome and laborious than the ascent"—at about 1:00 p.m., reaching camp by 4:00 p.m. "At five o'clock, in company with Miss Dickinson and Mr. Meeker, we set out for Evans' ranch in Estes park, twelve miles away, and reached that place in three hours," the writer concluded. The Hayden party followed later that evening.

Nothing in this detailed account suggests that Dickinson was the first woman to summit Longs Peak, but she soon became known for this feat, and there is no evidence to suggest that she attempted to refute the claim. It's entirely likely that she did not know that others had preceded her; it's equally likely that she hoped this notoriety would help to reenergize her flagging speaking career. She cannot be to blame, then, for Enos Mills's recommendation that a mountain be named for her within the park many years later—a comparatively smaller peak at 11,836 feet.

It does not seem that Dickinson got the boosted fame she sought after her climb. The lecture circuit dwindled in general as people found other forms of entertainment, and she eventually turned to acting, a profession that did not serve her well. Her income dried up, and she found herself living with friends, and eventually she spent time in mental institutions in the Catskill region of upstate New York. Her friends must have done their best for her, however, as she lived to see her ninetieth year and died in 1932.

"DRAGGED UP, LIKE A BALE OF GOODS"

While Anna Dickinson explored the land near Estes Park and made herself part of a climbing party, Isabella Bird was on her way to Colorado. An Englishwoman in her early forties, she had made travel and adventure part of her life from a young age, first on a sea voyage for her health and later of her own volition, with the United States and Canada her first

An unknown artist captured this portrait of Isabella Bird.
LIBRARY OF CONGRESS

destinations. She had lived with the people of the West Highlands of Scotland to assist their emigration to Canada, traveled to the lands along the Mediterranean Sea, and just completed an extended period of travel to the Sandwich Islands—what we know as Hawaii.

The Rocky Mountains became her next destination of choice, and she crossed the Pacific Ocean to San Francisco to begin her journey eastward, relieved to be free of the crowded streets and stifling heat she met with in California. She took a train to Truckee, in the Sierra Mountains, visited Lake Tahoe, and continued east by train to Fort Collins, where she managed to get a ride on a horse-drawn wagon to a rude boardinghouse. The sad little hovel, the property of a family named Chalmers somewhere past the east end of Big Thompson Canyon, was a structure so poorly maintained that Bird referred to it as an "open shed."

Here she found herself stranded for days, pitching into the work of running the homestead and sleeping on a straw mattress, some nights dragging it outside into the open air. She made a point of meeting everyone who lived nearby, many of them emigrants with no resources and others who had come from the eastern states for their health and now found themselves living in wagons or shanties. In the interim, she fought off swarms of black flies and other biting insects, killed a rattlesnake "and have taken its rattle, which has eleven joints," and busied herself with mending, knitting, and the many tasks of taking care of herself in a place where no one had the time or inclination to provide for her.

Finally, she persuaded Mr. Chalmers to provide her with a horse to take her through the canyon to Estes Park and the mountains beyond. She donned her "Hawaiian riding dress"—a short jacket, ankle-length skirt, and Turkish trousers that gathered in folds around her boots—and made her way to Longmont, where she stayed with a family who had a house next to a rushing stream. This family "indicates who should not come to Colorado," she noted, as they had no useful skills when they arrived and illness threatened their well-being. After weeks of waiting for an opportunity to get further into the Rocky Mountain wilderness, she finally despaired and began making plans to head to Denver, and from there to New York, when another visitor connected her with two young men who planned to ride into Estes Park the following day.

Bird never names the two men with whom she would traverse the canyon and later climb a mountain, but other historians have noted that they were Sylvester Spelman Downer, who later became a judge in Boulder, and Platt Rogers, who would one day become mayor of Denver. Perhaps her reticence to name them has to do with their general disinterest in having her, a woman, along for their own adventure in the Wild West, and with their treatment of her as a nuisance and a hindrance throughout most of their time together. Rogers later wrote an account of this arrangement for Enos Mills's book, *The Story of Estes Park and a Guide Book*: "We were not at all partial to such an arrangement as we were traveling light and free and the presence of a woman would naturally operate as a restraint upon our movements. However, we could not refuse"; and he goes on to note that her plain appearance, "with a face and figure not corresponding to our ideals," made her all the less interesting to them.

Three days later, the disdain of her escorts notwithstanding, Bird was in Estes Park and free of the miserable accommodations and the malaise they had caused. She had a clean, well-appointed cabin to herself on the Griffith Evans ranch, jovial hosts, plenty of fresh food, and scenery, which "is the most glorious I have ever seen, and is above us, around us, at the very door."

On the way through the canyon with her two companions, she came upon another precarious shack, but this one's occupant intrigued her above everyone else she had met in Colorado. Known as "Rocky Mountain Jim," he had lost an eye in a battle with a grizzly bear and lived as a recluse at the canyon bottom, but his manners and speech were genteel and clearly English, and he charmed Isabella immediately. A few days later, he became the guide who saw to it that she would reach the summit of Longs Peak.

She and the two young men with whom she had ridden through the canyon joined Jim, who "was a shocking figure; he had on an old pair of high boots, with a baggy pair of old trousers made of deer hide, held on by an old scarf tucked into them; a leather shirt, with three or four ragged unbuttoned waistcoats over it; an old smashed wideawake, from under which his tawny, neglected ringlets hung; and with his one eye, his one long spur, his knife in his belt, his revolver in his waistcoat pocket,

"Rocky Mountain Jim" Nugent's cabin stood somewhere in this canyon.
LIBRARY OF CONGRESS

his saddle covered with an old beaver skin, from which the paws hung down; his camping blankets behind him, his rifle laid across the saddle in front of him, and his axe, canteen, and other gear hanging to the horn, he was as awful-looking a ruffian as one could see." He surprised her entirely, however, with his ability to carry on a conversation like a man of letters, and they chatted for hours as they rode toward the tree line on Longs Peak.

In camp that night, she observed, "though his manner was certainly bolder and freer than that of gentlemen generally, no imaginary fault could be found. He was very agreeable as a man of culture as well as a child of nature; the desperado was altogether out of sight. He was very courteous and even kind to me, which was fortunate, as the young men had little idea of showing even ordinary civilities."

The next day, the climb began with a sunrise that impressed Bird so much that she noted, "I felt as if, Parsee-like, I must worship." The party started up the mountain in below-freezing temperatures, leaving their outer clothing behind despite the chill, and soon Isabella found herself struggling with the thin mountain air, her too-large borrowed boots, and the daunting task of crossing expanses of smooth vertical slabs of rock, rising pinnacles, and fields of unbroken snow.

She stopped to take in the view from the Notch and became nearly overwhelmed by the sight. "Serrated ridges, not much lower than that on which we stood, rose, one beyond another, far as that pure atmosphere could carry the vision, broken into awful chasms deep with ice and snow, rising into pinnacles piercing the heavenly blue with their cold, barren grey, on, on for ever [sic], till the most distant range upbore unsullied snow alone. There were fair lakes mirroring the dark pine woods, canyons dark and blue-black with unbroken expanses of pines, snow slashed pinnacles, wintry heights from frowning upon lovely parks, watered and wooded, lying in the lap of summer. . . . Never-to-be-forgotten glories they were, burnt in upon my memory by six succeeding hours of terror."

Somehow in her zeal to reach this mountain, Bird had not absorbed the fact that this was a climb and not a hike—something that every ranger in the park emphasizes to would-be mountaineers today. "I have no head and no ankles, and never ought to dream of mountaineering; and had I known that the ascent was a real mountaineering feat I should not have felt the slightest ambition to perform it," she confided in her book. "As it is, I am only humiliated by my success, for 'Jim' dragged me up, like a bale of goods, by sheer force of muscle."

She described the climb from the Notch to the top, crossing two thousand feet of rock, ribs of ice-rimed granite, and refrozen melted snow. Before long it became clear that the route they were on had been made impassable by the early fall snows, and Bird all but begged to be left behind at the Notch while the men made for the top, but Jim would have none of it. "The trapper replied shortly that if it were not to take a lady up he would not go up at all," she wrote, and soon they began to work their way down to a different route, spending two hours crawling down the slick rock faces. "My fatigue, giddiness, and pain from bruised ankles, and arms half pulled out of their sockets, were so great that I should never have gone halfway had not 'Jim,' *nolens volens*, dragged me along with a patience and skill, and withal a determination that I should ascend the Peak, which never failed."

Finally they reached the Dog's Lift, a passage between two huge rocks, and came out onto a narrow ledge that seemed like a broad floor to Bird's exhausted body. "As we crept from the ledge round a horn of rock I beheld what made me perfectly sick and dizzy to look at—the terminal Peak itself—a smooth, cracked face or wall of pink granite, as nearly perpendicular as anything could well be up which it was possible to climb, well deserving the name of the 'American Matterhorn,'" she said. Another hour's climb took them up the last five hundred feet, with them stopping and gasping for breath every few minutes in the frosty, high-altitude air, "but at last the Peak was won. A grand, well-defined mountain top it is, a nearly level acre of boulders, with precipitous sides all round, the one we came up being the only accessible one."

For reasons of their own, they had carried no water on their climb, so now, plagued by thirst and nearly blue with cold, with one man coughing up blood, they could not linger long at the top. The descent seemed far easier to Bird, accompanied as she was by Jim down the longer but somewhat safer route, while the two young men descended on a faster but more difficult course. Bird stumbled and fell several times, "and once hung by my frock, which caught on a rock, and 'Jim' severed it with his hunting knife, upon which I fell into a crevice full of soft snow," she reported. "Sometimes I drew myself up on hands and knees, sometimes crawled; sometimes 'Jim' pulled me up by my arms or a lariat, and sometimes I stood on his shoulders, or he made steps for me of his feet and hands, but at six we stood on the 'Notch' in the splendor of the sinking sun, all color deepening, all peaks glorifying, all shadows purpling, all peril past."

They reached their horses soon after and rode to their campsite, and in the morning, they returned to Estes Park. Despite feeling that she had misjudged the mountain and reached its apex in a way that did not truly suit her independent spirit, Bird accepted the reality of her accomplishment. "A more successful ascent of the Peak was never made," she concluded, perhaps with the giddy delusion of someone who has completed her first climb, as daunting as it had proved to be, "and I would not now exchange my memories of its perfect beauty and extraordinary sublimity for any other experience of mountaineering in any part of the world."

Isabella Bird remained in the Rocky Mountains until December 12, deepening her relationship with Rocky Mountain Jim. She never returned to Colorado, in part because of Jim's fate not long after she left (more on this in the chapter on "The Killing of Mountain Jim"), but she traveled abroad to much of Europe, the Pacific Rim, and the Middle East, and her travels made her such an expert in geography and foreign affairs that she became the first female member of the Royal Geographical Society in England.

Tragedy on the East Face:
The Death of Agnes Vaille

This shelter commemorates
a Colorado mountaineer
conquered by winter after
scaling the precipice
January 12, 1925
And one who lost his life
in an effort to aid her
Herbert Sortland
—PLAQUE AT AGNES VAILLE SHELTER, LONGS PEAK

IT TAKES A CERTAIN KIND OF PERSON TO LOOK UP AT THE TALLEST mountain in Rocky Mountain National Park, sort out the various routes to the summit, and decide to take on one of the most difficult—the East Face. More than ten thousand people summit Longs Peaks annually these days, the vast majority of whom follow the nontechnical Keyhole Route in July and August when climbers are least likely to encounter snow. Taking the path of least resistance satisfies most hikers, as well it should—the five-thousand-foot change in elevation from the trailhead to the peak leads climbers to struggle with altitude sickness, sudden storms and lightning, frigid temperatures, and fatigue that saps their strength, and that's on what some experienced climbers call the "easy" route.

The East Face, however, presents its own set of challenges, enough to earn it a Yosemite Decimal System rating of Class 4, Grade II, with ratings as high as 5.9 for specific rock climbs. Beginning with a hike around Chasm Lake, the route gets progressively steeper as climbers pass over Mills Glacier and into the Lamb's Slide couloir, a rocky route with pockets of ice even in July; this leads to a series of narrow ledges known, with characteristic irony, as Broadway. Snow on the Broadway ledges never melts away completely, so climbers encounter ice here along an eight-hundred-foot drop-off, followed by a crossing to the landmark known as the Notch Couloir (not to be confused with the Keyhole, which early climbers sometimes called the Notch). From here the climb becomes technical, requiring ropes and the use of pitons established by previous climbers. The last ice-covered section before the summit requires climbers to carve steps in the snow or to use the steps carved by other parties that may have passed through recently. It's a hard day's climb that begins before dawn, and the descent may be every bit as challenging as reaching the top.

If you have managed to assemble a picture in your mind of this route up the East Face, let's add another level of difficulty: Imagine climbing it in a blizzard.

Walter Kiener and Agnes Vaille spent the better part of the winter of 1924–25 attempting to master this climb, leaving enough of an impression on history that this trek is now known as Kiener's Route. A native of Switzerland who had considerable experience climbing in the Alps, Kiener moved to Denver around 1923, worked as a butcher, and became a member of the Colorado Mountain Club, often climbing with Vaille, who served as the club's outing chairperson.

Agnes was no ordinary young woman. At thirty-five years old, she had a well-established business career as appointed secretary to the Denver Chamber of Commerce, a Smith College education, and a record of travel to Paris during World War I to volunteer for the Red Cross there. She earned her reputation as a mountaineer by taking on a number of peaks around her home in Boulder and elsewhere in Colorado, and according to Janet Robertson's book, *The Magnificent Mountain Women*, she was "one of the state's earliest female technical climbers."

Longs Peak's Keyhole and other routes to the summit had become popular climbs for visitors to Rocky Mountain National Park, but only

Agnes Vaille climbed mountains in a long skirt and high lace-up boots, as was the custom of the day. HISTORY COLORADO

one woman—Elmira Buhl—had traversed the East Face to reach the summit so far, in September 1922. Vaille had strong rock-climbing capabilities and at least one "first" to her own credit, a summit of James Peak in winter. She and Kiener joined a climbing party in early fall 1924 with Herman and Elmira Buhl, and together they summited Mount Evans at 14,265 feet, just a few feet higher than Longs (at 14,259 feet). Elmira must have described her climb up the East Face that day, because Vaille and Kiener became intrigued by the prospect of duplicating her achievement. As snow and cold arrived in the fall of 1924, they decided to attempt their own precedent-setting climb: the East Face in winter, a season that even the most skilled climbers among the club's members had not attempted.

Their first try took place in October, before the winter's heaviest snowfall, but they encountered plenty of ice as they made their way up. Then Kiener dropped his ice axe, an error that could easily have led to a deadly fall from the ice if he had no way of arresting a slide. He informed Vaille that they had to turn back, and she did not question his judgment, following her Colorado Mountain Club training to obey the leader in all

Agnes Vaille was a veteran mountain climber with many successes to her credit.
NATIONAL PARK SERVICE

cases. By this time, they had to make their way down the ice in darkness, giving them a good idea of what the process would be like if they chose to pursue this goal later in the winter.

Undaunted, they planned another ascent in November, apparently unconcerned about the difference between weather in October and the potential gales, blizzards, and precipitous drops in temperature they could encounter on the exposed rock faces in late fall. Vaille got in touch with her friend Carl Blaurock, one of the most respected mountain climbers in the region, and asked to borrow his ice axe. "He was horrified to hear that she was going to try the climb in a season when storms could come up quickly and temperatures plunge dangerously without warning," Robertson wrote in her book, based on an unpublished manuscript dictated by Walter Kiener to friend Charles Edwin Hewes. When Blaurock could not convince Vaille that she was taking her life in her hands, and because he was most familiar with the mountain, he offered to come with her and Kiener.

This time, they nearly made it to the summit, but the route they chose slowed down their progress enough that they would have to complete the climb and descend in pitch darkness. The descent took so long that they had to rush back to Denver just to get to work on time on Monday, making their failure to reach the summit even more frustrating. Vaille and Kiener were ready to plan another attempt, but Blaurock declined to accompany them if they planned to do so in winter.

In December, with winter well established, Vaille and Kiener planned their third try, but weather kept them from getting very far at all. "By now Agnes's friends and relatives regarded her desire to climb the East Face in winter as an 'obsession,'" Robertson noted. So many of these people insisted to her that the climb was too dangerous that she dug in her heels, becoming even more determined to proceed regardless of the warnings and admonitions. Even Kiener claimed in his account to Hewes that he attempted to talk Vaille out of another climb.

Nonetheless, the afternoon of January 10, 1925, found them driving through ice and snowdrifts toward Longs Peak with their friend Elinor Eppich going along for the ride, their vehicle sliding on the ice and finally stopping altogether when the snow on the road became too deep to navigate. Here they donned skis, loaded up their supplies, and skied the rest of the way to the Longs Peak Inn and Timberline Cabin, where they arrived in the wee hours of the morning. They spent a chilly night, with wind and snow coming through the cracks in the walls.

In the morning, gale force winds made the party certain that there would be no climb that day—but suddenly the wind died, the clouds parted, and Longs Peak stood out clearly against the crystal blue sky. Kiener would later tell Hewes that Vaille was "enthusiastic" about starting their ascent, while Eppich wrote that Kiener not only insisted that they make the climb but tried hard to persuade Eppich, who had no boots or climbing gear with her, to join them for the trek. In an unpublished manuscript discovered by Robertson, Eppich did her best to set the record straight as rumors and suppositions circulated that "it was all Agnes's stubbornness and poor judgment that were responsible for the whole tragedy. That simply is not so."

It was already 9:00 a.m., too late in the morning for a successful summit before dark. Normally the climbing party would have left well before dawn, but their late arrival at Timberline Cabin—one account says they got there at 3:00 a.m.—gave them little time to sleep before they started out.

Kiener and Vaille headed for Chasm Lake and began the climb, making the most of the bright, sunny conditions, but when the early sunset found them only partway up the mountain, they had a critical decision to make. Continuing upward could take them many hours, and they could not stay at the summit and wait for daylight to come down, because temperatures had already plunged with the fading light. Turning around and heading down meant admitting defeat once again, though that would be preferable to risking their lives to the cold and fatigue. Kiener already recognized that Vaille had lost much of her energy and her strength was "about spent." As the leader of their expedition, he had a critical decision to make.

"We decided we'd just as well go up, as we would have to make the descent in the dark," Kiener told the media two days later. He noted later that they achieved the summit at about 4:00 a.m. Monday morning: "Arrived at the top we didn't tarry—we started downward immediately." He checked his thermometer at the summit, and found that the mercury had sunk to fourteen degrees below zero. They had a long way to go, and the weather was getting worse.

Rather than go back the precarious way they had come, Kiener got his bearings during a break in the cloud bank that swirled around them and led them down the Cables route, a well-established and somewhat shorter route that had led many climbers to a successful summit. Later that year, the park installed steel cables to assist climbers in navigating to the top, but when Kiener chose it as his return route, it had no such guide wires. He and Vaille stumbled down the route as best they could, but by this time, Vaille's strength had flagged to the point where she had difficulty continuing to move. Her feet and hands were numb with frostbite. "We were coming down a slope when Miss Vaille slipped," Kiener went on. "She slid and rolled 150 feet down before she stopped. She wasn't hurt physically, but after the hardships, it unnerved her. We continued. . . . 'I can't go on,' she declared."

It's interesting to note at this point that in the account Kiener told to Charles Hewes, he said that he asked Vaille if she could go on, and "she nodded in the affirmative."

He tried to carry her, but his own endurance had limits, and soon they were both prostrate in the snow. Kiener dragged Vaille to the shelter of a large boulder and left her there while he descended the rest of the way. He fell and fell again, but eventually, through blowing snow, he could see the outline of Timberline Cabin, and he called out to whoever might be nearby.

"Just as I managed to get within calling distance, I went down," he said.

He'd gone far enough to save his own life, however. By this time, it was 1:00 p.m. on Monday afternoon, and Eppich, knowing that the pair had to be in trouble on the mountain, had assembled a rescue party, who were ready to start a search. Hearing of Vaille's precarious condition, they left immediately, "fighting every inch of the way through a blinding snowstorm," the *Nebraska State Journal* reported.

TRAGEDY COMPOUNDED

Herbert Sortland, who was twenty-three, was one of the members of the rescue party. Caretaker of the Longs Peak Inn, he had joined the group, which included Hugh Brown and his son, Oscar Brown, and Jacob Christen, and was ready to head out into the gale to find Kiener, had he not reappeared, and the suffering Agnes Vaille.

By sheer force of will, Kiener gathered his last strength and began to lead the party to the Boulderfield, where he had left Vaille. Oscar Brown stayed behind, and soon Sortland and Hugh Brown realized that they did not have the proper clothing and equipment to negotiate their way through the weather or up the icy mountain. Brown left first, following his own trail back to Timberline, and soon Sortland followed him. Christen and Kiener continued on to the Boulderfield.

When they arrived at the boulder where Kiener had left Vaille, they found that she had frozen to death. They attempted to lift her to bring

Vaille and Kiener were close to the Boulderfield when Vaille could go no farther.
NATIONAL PARK SERVICE

her down with them, but Kiener had no strength to spare, and Christen had exhausted himself just getting to this place in the snow and wind. In the end, they knew that since the time for rescue had passed, there was no urgency requiring them to risk their own lives to bring Vaille down. They made their way back down to the cabin. Christen took the lead and assisted Kiener, who by this time could barely stand—his hands and feet were frozen nearly solid. They fought blindly through whiteout conditions, using wind direction like a compass point until they managed to reach Timberline Cabin at about 7:30 p.m.

When they arrived, they found the Browns but no Sortland. A search party went out the following day, but they found no sign of him, and by the end of the day they knew that any further effort would be to find only the young man's body.

"Then at intervals struggled in men whom the drifts and gale and flying snow and bitter cold of the winter night could not keep back," said an account by John Dickinson Sherman, editor of the *Chicago Herald* as well as the Western Newspaper Union, which appeared in dozens of papers across the country.

Each had started as the news reached him that Agnes Vaille was in danger on Longs Peak. By 10 o'clock had arrived Tom Allen, assistant superintendent of the park, and Jack Moomaw and Walter Finn, park rangers. At 4:30 Tuesday morning Superintendent Roger W. Toll (cousin of Agnes Vaille) arrived from Denver, with Edmund Rogers, George C. Barnard, William F. Ervin and Carl Blaurock, veteran mountaineers of the Colorado Mountain club. Daylight found them all trying to keep from freezing about a fire kept burning on top of the cabin stove. To recover Agnes Vaille's body was impossible. At 9:30 all descended to the valley. . . . Not until Thursday could Agnes Vaille's body be reached. It lay at an elevation of about 13,300 feet on the north slope, 200 feet back of the edge of the East Face, and about 50 feet above the perpetual snowdrift on the edge of Boulderfield. . . . Two skis were placed end to end and a third lashed across the joint. The body was strapped to these skis and carried with the aid of ski poles. Eight men carried the body across Boulderfield, relays taking part at frequent intervals. Further down a toboggan could be used.

Six weeks would pass before the body of Herbert Sortland finally came to light, just about three hundred yards from the Longs Peak Inn, where he had fallen and apparently dislocated a hip. Unable to walk, he succumbed to the elements on the edge of a frozen swamp near the inn's garbage dump, where Oscar Brown happened upon him while bringing a load to the dump on February 25, 1925.

Kiener's survival of the incident did not bring him comfort for some time after the ordeal that took his friend's life. He himself lost most of his toes and several fingers, leaving him unable to continue his career as a butcher, the only trade he had learned when he left school at fifteen to apprentice with his father as a sausage maker in Bern. The Vaille family, who were well off enough to assist the young man, paid all of his medical expenses as well as his tuition to attend the University of Nebraska.

71

He majored in botany and eventually earned a doctorate, which led the university to hire him as an assistant in botany, a position he held for ten years. He then became a biologist with the Nebraska Game, Forestation and Parks Commission, where he rose to the position of chief biologist and established the commission's Fisheries Research Department. He died of pancreatic cancer in 1959, leaving an extensive library of more than fifty thousand plant samples that are now in the Charles E. Bessey Herbarium at the University of Nebraska.

In 1927, Vaille's family also made a donation to the park to construct a monument to Agnes on Longs Peak. The Agnes Vaille Memorial Shelter stands at 13,400 feet, with a fireplace, wood, and food inside for anyone who may be stranded on the mountain. "It's used all the time," Karen Waddell, cultural resources specialist at the park, told the *Daily Camera* in 2013. If it has saved even one life, the Vailles' well-placed generosity has done its job for adventurers who choose to take themselves to the limits of their own endurance on one of the most challenging mountains in Colorado.

The Quest for Gold and Silver

Great uncertainty is a necessary condition of gold-hunting. While one man "does well" from the start, there will always be many others, equally worthy and industrious, who are less fortunate. In California and Australia, not more than one in ten of all the immigrants have been successful. Under the most favorable circumstances, even after a rich "lead" is discovered, digging gold is one of the hardest kinds of manual labor in the world. Men who are hardy, energetic, self-reliant and persevering, *may reasonably expect, sooner or later, a fair reward for their labors. Those who are timid, wavering and easily discouraged, should by all means remain at home.*

—A. D. Richardson
Milwaukee Daily Sentinel, March 29, 1860

It began with dust—a handful of yellow powder in Cherry Creek where it joins the South Platte River—revealing itself to George Simpson in May 1857. Soon Fall Leaf, a Native American of the Delaware tribe, came across some gold nuggets in an area that would become the city of Denver. In 1858, William Green Russell, a white man from Georgia with a Cherokee wife, heard that Cherokees had come across gold dust in a tributary of the South Platte River nearly a decade before, so he headed west with his brothers and Cherokee tribe members in May, and they toiled until they found gold at the mouth of Little Dry Creek (now the town of Englewood) and even more to the south, past Cherry Creek.

The news of a new gold strike in the western mountains reached eastern newspapers, and wagon trains began to roll westward, filled with

Burros carried in supplies and carried out gold dust. LIBRARY OF CONGRESS

people to whom life had not dealt a winning hand. Farmers whose crops had failed that summer, debt-ridden city dwellers, and laborers struggling to make ends meet saw new promise in the possibility of a quickly amassed fortune. First, hundreds of people came, and then, when the papers reported that some prospectors had struck pay dirt, thousands more loaded up their families and headed for the Rocky Mountains. The events had stirred a longing in fortune-seekers in the United States, drawing their attention westward to what they believed might be easy money in their pockets.

The *Chicago Tribune* noted the departure of one such group of sixteen men in March 1860: "The largest company that has yet, this season, left Chicago for that destination, started yesterday for Pike's Peak. . . . The party, as many of our city readers will discern, comprises gentlemen of

Miners had to be hardy individuals to take on the demanding work inside their mines. LIBRARY OF CONGRESS

spirit, energy, and enterprise. They go out to El Dorado duly 'armed and equipped' at all points of outfit, as well as in experience and character to make their mark in the new communities they will seek. . . . They carry with them mules, wagons, tents and provisions, with which they strike out westward from St. Joseph. The company will thoroughly prospect the streams rising in the South Park. They go with provisions for six months. They go with an intelligent purpose and will not easily be disheartened."

A month later, the western movement dwarfed the size of this Chicago caravan, as the *Tribune* reported, "We learn from the Omaha

(Nebraska) *Republican* that 221 men, having with them 75 wagons, crossed the ferry at that place, on their way for Pike's Peak, from April 4 to April 10, inclusive—one week."

By early 1859, towns in Missouri and Kansas became jammed with prospectors buying up wagons, oxen, mining tools, flour, coffee, smoked meat, and anything else they believed they would need, and roads—mostly just ruts in the earth from the weight of thousands of wagon wheels—became clogged with carts and horses as eager miners made their way to the land of promise.

The Colorado Gold Rush—often called the Pikes Peak Gold Rush after the familiar landmark, though mining did not begin in earnest near that peak until the 1890s—changed the shape and economy of Colorado forever, leading to the construction of cities, including Denver, Boulder, and Golden, and placing the territory on track to becoming a state. Its effects reached far beyond the purses of a few lucky prospectors, changing the balance of power in the territory and bringing a new population of young, energetic men, the vast majority of them white, native-born American emigrants, into the West.

Just ten years after prospectors rushed to California to mine the gold discovered there, this second discovery of gold in the West occurred largely along the South Platte River, in the mountains west of Golden, and in South Park ("park" in Colorado refers to an upland valley). Prospectors sought the gold that came to the surface in stream beds—what is known as placer mining—and quickly stripped out the precious metal they found by excavating at the bottom of creeks and in open pits, using rocker boxes to sift gold dust out of the wet gravel and sand under the water.

"The winning of the gold from the gravel was the simplest process that could be used in mining," wrote E. J. Garbella, a second lieutenant in the Army Corps of Engineers Reserve, in an article in the *Military Engineer* journal in 1932. "Very little apparatus was needed, and this could be of the crudest kind. The gold recovered was of course in the native state—it was the glittering yellow metal that was so precious. It could be easily carried, and its value was great per unit of weight."

Placer mining, however, soon ran dry, and digging lode mines with shovels and picks became the backbreaking work of the ambitious miner.

If a mine shaft produced signs of gold ore, miners could use this find to buy equipment to dig deeper and farther into the earth. "When men working the gravels found they could make more money on lodes, they of course deserted the placers," Garbella said. "Some placer activity persisted on a large scale, and at various places in Colorado a person can see the results of former activity—great piles of rocks that have been worked over by dredges, and sometimes even dredges are left, idle and rotting away. Many of the deposits were worked out—that is, they became poor, making it impossible to save gold at a profit, and some of the dredging companies were forced to quit because of litigation arising because of the pollution of the streams by the dredges."

Colorado needed some rules, so it began to operate under the same mining claim laws established a decade earlier in California and soon developed its own mining laws for the territory. Prospectors could stake claims of 1,500 feet long by 150 to 600 feet wide, depending on the local laws of the specific territory, and each claim had to be marked, "a notice giving the boundaries and date of location left on the claim—and a copy filed at the county recorder's office—and a ten foot shaft dug into the mineral bearing ledge," said Robert Spude, a historian with the National Park Service, in an unpublished manuscript in 1990. "Also, a claim stake

Placer mining took place on the surface, using water to separate gold flakes from the soil. LIBRARY OF CONGRESS

Miners were required by law to tunnel ten feet into their property to maintain the claim. LIBRARY OF CONGRESS

with the discovery notice was posted, trees blazed or piles of stones erected to mark corners."

Just identifying the boundaries of the claim was not enough to denote ownership, however. "To hold the claim, $100 worth of work on the mine or $500 work of improvements to the area was required each year—the 'annual assessment,'" said Spude. "If the work was not performed, the claim reverted to federal ownership and was available for others to stake. In general, the amount of work was loosely interpreted to mean two weeks in the mine or the erection of a cabin."

During the summer of 1859, some twenty-five thousand of the possible fifty thousand gold seekers who headed for Colorado went into the

Front Range mountains. The truth about gold in the region soon came to the surface, however—only a few of the miners saw the kind of luck so many sought, and tens of thousands of disappointed "go-backers" gave up and began to head east once again. Those who stayed moved deeper into the territory, and their luck improved: Soon they discovered significant supplies of gold in the Gregory region, at the North Fork of Clear Creek. "Prospectors became possessed by 'Gregory Fever,'" the *Colorado Encyclopedia* tells us. "Early that month the wooded slopes of Gregory Gulch sheltered a population of 4,000 or 5,000 that slept in tents or lean-to shelters of pine boughs. Over the next month 500 newcomers arrived daily."

One of these newcomers was Joel Estes, the man who lent his name to the area we now know as Estes Park. Born in Kentucky and established as a Missouri farmer, he and the oldest of his thirteen children, Hardin, ran westward for the California gold rush in 1849 and came back with a tidy sum of more than thirty thousand dollars for their trouble, but this apparently only whetted their appetites for riches. Estes and various members of his family sought other opportunities in California and the Pacific Northwest in the 1850s and finally decided to settle briefly in the Rocky Mountains to try their luck with the new gold rush.

They arrived in Denver in June 1859 and quickly sized up the mining situation for what it was. Estes decided instead to look for the best place to graze his herd of cattle, following advice to look at a place called Fort Lupton Bottom, a hidden valley at the end of a twenty-mile-long canyon. When he arrived there with his son, Milton, the two of them were instantly smitten. They departed for the winter and returned in 1860 to build cabins on the land they had decided to make their own, becoming "squatters" in a territory where possession became law. Estes himself tended to his affairs in Missouri and Denver, but he hired hands to see to his cattle and harvest the game animals that were plentiful throughout the region, which provided them with meat and hides for their own use as well as products to take to market.

Estes and his family settled into their Colorado valley in 1863 and stayed until 1866; by then the harsh winters, lonely seasons, and rugged pioneer life had taken their toll. The family packed up and moved into southern Colorado. "Scenery and good hunting were no match for rough winters and loneliness," observed historian C. W. Buchholtz in his book, *Rocky Mountain National Park: A History*. Before they decided to move on, however, they received a visit from William N. Byers, editor of the *Rocky Mountain News*, who was so impressed with the Estes family's estate that he wrote of it in his newspaper, referring to the land as "Estes Park." The name took permanent hold and remains on the park's most popular entrance town to this day.

THE INEVITABLE CLASH

With such an enormous influx of young white men into the territory, confrontations with the Native American population became unavoidable. The plains had been the home of native Arapaho, Cheyenne, Kiowa, and Sioux peoples; the Utes lived in the mountains; and all of the tribes moved down into the Platte River valley in fall and winter, when weather on the windswept prairie and in the high peaks became too rough. Years before, in 1851, the Cheyenne and Arapaho had signed the Treaty of Fort Laramie with the US government, making the lands from Fort Laramie, Wyoming, south to Big Sandy Creek—the northeastern quarter of what would become the state of Colorado—the property of the native peoples in perpetuity. Cheyenne and Arapaho continued to live in this region as the Cheyenne had for centuries (the Arapaho had arrived much more recently), migrating with the seasons, hunting buffalo and other game, and gathering what they needed from the grasslands and forests. In return for being left to their own devices on this land, the native people gave safe passage to settlers making their way across the plains and the mountains on the Oregon Trail.

Suddenly, in the winter of 1858–59, it became clear that much of the gold that interested the Anglo Americans resided on and under Native American land. The Cheyenne and Arapaho encountered white men who had staked claims, marked their own territories, and set up boundaries all over the land the treaty had guaranteed to the native people. The white newcomers had no interest in sharing this land with "Indians," nor did they regard the native people's needs for buffalo hunting or firewood to be any of their concern. The new arrivals consumed precious resources and left little for those who had lived off the land for centuries. Equally troublesome, they paid no attention to the boundaries set by the Treaty of Fort Laramie, considering themselves entitled to all of the land in this US territory.

The Native Americans resorted to raiding white mining camps and wagon trains, taking what food they could and doing their best to scare these interlopers into going home. As they defended their homeland, however, they also fought a more insidious foe: diseases brought by white settlers, against which they had no natural immunity. They succumbed to smallpox, measles, tuberculosis, and influenza, all felling their numbers more effectively than armies and guns could.

The situation had become untenable, so the US government dispatched Commissioner of Indian Affairs Alfred Burton Greenwood to the territory to negotiate a new treaty with the Cheyenne and Arapaho. Despite objections from the leaders of both tribes, the new Treaty of Fort Wise established a much smaller reservation on the Upper Arkansas River, in which the native people would give up hunting and gathering, the lifestyle that had sustained them for centuries, and become farmers. The US government would provide them with the tools and resources they needed to make this fairly dramatic transition, but the Cheyenne and Arapaho would relinquish the land throughout the Front Range and the plains, leaving it open to gold mining by the Anglo Americans.

The chiefs signed this treaty on February 15, 1861, but they did not realize that by doing so, they were signing away their land and lifestyle. In fact, many Cheyenne and Arapaho people continued to live as before, hunting buffalo on the plains as best they could, as if no treaty had been signed and nothing had changed. Now the white miners believed themselves entitled to the land, so the clashes between settlers and tribespeople continued, escalating with the rise of the militaristic Cheyenne Dog Soldiers, who led the conflict against the American army.

Silver in Lulu City

This conflict with the local Native Americans amounted to a great deal of animosity for a very small gain. By the end of the first season of gold fever, many of the placer deposits had been exhausted, and as many as half of the fortune-seekers who had dashed to the region in the spring had packed up and headed homeward. Some had found gold "in varying quantities from the Arkansas River to the Cache la Poudre," wrote Robert Spude, but they had little luck in the area that would become Rocky Mountain National Park. A Wisconsin farmer named Alonzo Allen, for example, worked the Mammoth lode mine in the area now known as Allenspark, sharing the workload with three partners through the winter of 1864, but the mine failed and Allen went back to farming on his land in Longmont. The first wave of gold mining came to an end in the area shortly thereafter.

Meanwhile, miners in Clear Creek Canyon had discovered silver in 1864, but silver did not have the market value that gold enjoyed, so the find did not generate much interest. That changed in 1878, when the US Congress passed the Bland-Allison Act, which allowed silver to be used to make coins—in particular, silver dollars—and suddenly turned the metal into a precious one. The price of silver rose steadily, making mining of the metal profitable for the first time and increasing excitement about the potential for silver mining in Colorado. And when silver was found in Leadville, where both gold and lead mining already turned a tidy profit, thousands of fortune-seekers headed west once again to take advantage of the new opportunity.

Mining soon picked up once again in the Rocky Mountain National Park area, and one of the hubs of activity formed along the eastern base of the Never Summer Mountains. Named for the daughter of speculator Benjamin Burnett, Lulu City sprang up almost overnight and soon had several business establishments, including a combination hardware and drug store, a general store, and a barbershop, as well as more than forty residential cabins.

Squeaky Bob Wheeler, the proprietor of a tent and cabin resort in Grand Lake, remembered young Lulu well, according to author Mary Lyons Cairns, who wrote *Grand Lake: The Pioneers* in 1946. "Lulu Burnett was the most beautiful girl I ever saw," he told her. "She had jet black hair, black eyes, and a very white skin; her lips were rosy red, and they didn't have lipstick in those days." Cairns noted that Lulu Pass and Lulu Mountain were also named for her, but these landmarks received a name change after the 1914 visit by the Arapaho. They are now Thunder Pass and Thunder Mountain.

Cairns, herself a Grand Lake resident not long after the pioneer days, found old documents that told a little more of Lulu City's story. "The townsite was platted," she wrote. "It had 100 blocks with sixteen lots to the block. The streets were numbers from First to Nineteenth inclusive; avenues ran at right angles and were called Mountain, Trout, Riverside, and Ward." She discovered the patent establishing the townsite, signed by President Chester A. Arthur and recorded by L. Harrison of the General Land Office.

In July 1880, the *Fort Collins Courier* carried an optimistic letter from a newly arrived resident of the mining town, identified only as H. C., detailing the progress he could see on his arrival. "Stewart's road is now within six miles of Lulu and still coming, and it is to be hoped will get here soon, at least every one that has tried packing in grub on pack saddles hopes so," he wrote. "We had two assayers in here last week who are now over in the North Park picking up the balance of their 'kit' as they say they are going to make Lulu their headquarters from now on. They both agree in saying that the mineral in this section represents exactly the mineral found in the vicinity of Georgetown, Caribou, Black Hawk and Central, and they do not hesitate to predict a bright future for this camp, and indeed, I think there can be no longer any doubt."

Two weeks later, Stewart's toll road opened to light traffic, and those returning from Middle Park brought "cheering reports of the situation in the Lead Mountain district," the *Courier* reported. "From 200 to 300 prospectors are busily engaged in staking out and sinking down on their claims. Everybody is encouraged at the outlook and the utmost confidence prevails among all with regard to the future of the camp."

Soon the newspaper featured announcements by attorneys hawking real estate deals in the burgeoning mining town, proclaiming, "Now is the time to secure a lot in one of the most thriving mining camps in Colorado." A miners' store run by proprietors Churchill and Harrison opened in Lulu City, promising "A Good General Stock consisting of Miners' Hardware, Gents' Furnishing Goods, Blankets and Comforts, Drugs and Medicines, Boots and Shoes, Hats and Caps, Groceries &c."

"New arrivals are coming in to town at the rate of ten to fifteen per day," H. C. reported in mid-August. "Some improvements are noticeable. A.J. Godsmark has commenced building a store house 20 by 40 feet, to be used for a general stock of goods . . . Mr. Parkhurst has his restaurant and boarding house nearly completed. Others are finishing and building houses. All feel satisfied that Lulu will make a good lively town, and mountain district will be one of the richest mining districts in Colorado— This question seems to be settled and at rest." The sawmill turned out lumber at a great rate, providing the boards people needed to build their own cabins. Nothing but happy news came out of the mountain town as silver prospects continued to advance.

"The mining boom is sounding nearer," H. C. predicted on August 30, 1880. "New discoveries are being found every day, and some very good ones. . . . Blasts can be heard at any hour of the day from mines in hearing of Lulu City. The Rustic mine, owned by Stuart & Co., is now one of the richest properties of Lead mountain district. The Ruby, Southern, Cross, North Star and P. Wimple lodes are all promising mines. The Rattlers No. 1, 2 and 3, show the largest body of mineral of any claims I have yet been able to see." So certain of their prospects were the miners in Lulu City that they established a voting precinct, "which will enable us to look better to our interests in the coming election." The county commissioners voted to build a road from Lulu to Grand Lake, to "place us in direct communication with Denver, Boulder and Georgetown."

H. C. finished his report with an orgiastic flourish: "Many a heart will ere long beat fast with joy. Many a poor wife and child will meet husband and father, and thank God for his kind care and protection of the brave one who has risked so much in securing means whereby they may be happy. We all feel greatly pleased over the future prospects of Lulu City. We do not, neither do we intend to write any matters concerning our town but the truth."

Mrs. Thomas Johnston and her husband remembered well the times that they visited Lulu City, as she told Cairns. "When Rob was a baby I went to a dance up at Lulu with Tom," she said. "The place certainly was lively in those days. There was a big hotel—oh, it seemed awfully large to me—and that was where we danced. On the tables were fine linen, lovely silverware and sparkling glasses. Think how hard it must have been to get all those things in the mining camps over the awful roads of those days, with wagons and teams. They moved the tables out of the dining room for the dance."

Most miners headed into larger towns or back home for the winter, but the owners of the Rustic and Southern mines kept them working through the frigid season. "The latter vein is reported to be 7 feet between walls, and the ore by average assays runs 100 ounces in silver and from one to three ounces in gold per ton," the *Denver Republican* reported. "Work sufficient to hold location and prove title has been accomplished, and vigorous development will be prosecuted early in the spring."

A year passed, and then another. In May 1882, the *Courier* reported that "two of Lulu City's bonanza kings," Ben Dunshee and Frank Wenderberg, had arrived in Fort Collins to spread the word that "several rich strikes had been made during the winter." The Cross and Robinson mines were "producing paying ore," and Dunshee expected "to see more work done the coming summer than has ever been done before."

The *Grand Lake Prospector* picked up the story from here. "Rumor of a new and very rich strike in the Wolverine mine has reached here, but we have as yet failed to learn anything definite in regard to the matter," it said in December 1882. The following July, the mine still showed promise; Cairns tells us the *Prospector* reported, "Lulu at present promises to be the liveliest of the mining camps this summer."

A year later, a writer at Grand Lake's paper revisited Lulu City's progress, but this time the tone had changed. "John R. Brennan and Jack Henry, two of Lulu's old timers, arrived there a few days ago and have been down to pay Grand Lake a visit. They say that Lulu is in a very dilapidated condition with the exception of the mines, and they look as bright as ever. They have contracts on the Ptarmigan and several other lodes."

And then the papers stopped reporting about Lulu City. The next and last notice came on January 30, 1886: "Lulu has been discontinued as a post office."

The particulars of what happened did not become part of the public record—apparently the media of the time did not elevate the importance of bad news over good—but like so many other mining operations in the area, the mines around Lulu City did not produce the high-quality ore required to turn a profit. Cairns offers a bit more information from her interviews with prospectors of the day: "Silver ore was found in abundance near Lulu City, but it was of low grade and most of it did not pay to ship. Little gold was ever found in the ore mined there. There were a few placer mines near the town, in the fine sand of the North Fork of the Grand River which flowed through the valley to the west." One unnamed prospector said to her, "Some day you'll see nothing but a foot trail along this street. Raspberry bushes and spruce trees will be growing through the roof of the hotel yonder."

His words served as prophecy. In a matter of months, the budding mining hub housed nothing but tumbleweed, according to an article in the *Craig Empire-Courier* in 1938. "Lulu City, a ghost town in the northwestern section of [Rocky Mountain] national park, is an historical enigma which park officials would like to solve," the article said. "It existed a comparatively short time, hardly more than a year, dying when hopes for gold changed into despair along the valueless sands of the Colorado river flowing nearby. Quartz claims also proved worthless. . . . Unconfirmed reports say that possibly 1000 people lived there for a short time, leaving almost as quickly as they arrived when gold prospects failed."

The remains of the town had not fared well in the ensuing years, the paper continued. "A number of log cabins are standing with their roofs caved in and their walls collapsed, but still revealing old window openings and doors. A beaver has taken possession of one partially ruined cabin, while through the interior of most of the ruins, large spruce and fir trees are growing. Best preserved in the ghost town is an old log bear trap, which, even now, could be placed in operation with comparatively little trouble."

Cairns took a walk through the area in the 1940s and noted, "One sees abandoned prospect holes here and there, with rotting timbers at the tunnel entrances. In the ore dump from the Joseph Shipler mine are some lovely crystals. Nothing will grow on a mine dump." She took a moment to explain the bear trap: "When the trap was in use, a piece of meat attached to a wire was placed inside at the rear of the trap. The wire was also attached to the huge log door in such a way that the door would fall when the meat was disturbed by a bear. Thus the bear was trapped inside."

The last days of Lulu City have long since been forgotten. Its remains, however, stand as an iconic example of the boom-and-bust nature of the area's mining days, and they reflect the promise that prospectors felt as they laid eyes on veins of lead and silver in the granite beneath a towering mountain. Today a 3.5-mile hike north from the Colorado River trailhead off Trail Ridge Road will take visitors to the remains of Lulu City: a cemetery, the ruins of three cabins, and bits and pieces of other buildings that once stood in this remote spot on the river.

THE SECOND RUSH AND THE PUMPKIN ROLLERS

Boulder County and the surrounding area would see one more gold rush, this time at the turn of the twentieth century.

Prospector Robert Womack was a homesteader in 1890, his property standing smack in the middle of a larger tract owned by the Pike's Peak Land and Cattle Company. Range riders complained that their lives were endangered as they rode across this land because of the many holes that Womack dug and redug across the property in his search for gold he believed he would find there. One day, after yet another hole yielded no result, he decided to give up the search, when a steer from the Pike's Peak claim wandered too close to him, and he picked up a rock to throw at the animal. To his amazement, this rock felt heavier than any other in the area. He picked up another rock and broke this one open, and stared at the glistening center of a gold nugget. Rushing to the nearest assayer, he discovered that his find was worth $2,500 per ton.

Womack would be known for the rest of his life as the "father of Cripple Creek," as his discovery led to the establishment of one of the most successful mining camps in the West. He himself, however, sold off his claims and never struck it rich, despite continuing to work the mine well into his fifties, even in the week before a stroke left him largely paralyzed in 1904.

The 1890 find renewed interest in claims at the base of many mountains throughout the Front Range, including those in the future Rocky Mountain National Park. By 1895, when Cripple Creek became the most productive mine in Colorado, another gold rush brought thousands of people to the territory once again, with a significant number choosing land along the upper St. Vrain River for their lode-mining activity. Exactly how many people staked claims in this area may never be known, but the park has documented nineteen claims on the east side of the park in the Longs Peak Mining District, hastily organized around a claim discovered by Charles Gallagher and Albert Newton, who named it Snow Storm after the conditions in which they found it on February 21, 1896.

"By May a full scale rush was underway," said Robert Spude in his 1990 report. "The mining camp of Jamestown saw 100 miners per day pass through on the way to Allenspark; the Burlington Railroad offered special rates and instructions on how to reach the camp from the jump off point of Lyons; and two townsites were laid out."

At first, the news reports from Denver raved ecstatically about the new camp. "Many veterans . . . say that Allen's Park will turn out to be another Cripple Creek," one reporter gushed in the *Rocky Mountain News.* "Ore veins occur in ten to fifty foot wide copper formations . . . and Ore runs $4 to 200/ton."

Arriving prospectors staked several hundred claims in the Longs Peak Mining District. By this time, Boulder County operated under a mining law that restricted claims to 1,500 feet long by 150 feet wide—slimmer than the 1872 federal statutes—and every claim had to be filed at the county recorder's office, its boundaries marked, and "a ten-foot shaft dug into the mineral-bearing ledge," said Spude. "For six miles around Allenspark, the former home of cowboy and coyote was now a mess of pits, stone piles and blazed trees."

This infuriated Enos Mills, mountain-climbing guide and future proprietor of the Longs Peak Inn, who in a decade would become the park's greatest champion. "What a terrible plague is gold fever!" he wrote at the time. "There are thousands of claims, and like lottery tickets, most of them are not only worthless but expensive. The piles of worthless rock dug out of valueless claims are but monuments of wasted work; while the stakes marking their boundaries are standing like headstones above buried hope."

What sustained this activity from one year to the next, especially as claim after claim turned up nothing more than dirt and rock? Investors from Nebraska—whom the local media called "pumpkin rollers"—found the mining game endlessly stimulating, according to Spude. "Colorado was a haven for wildcat speculation," he wrote. "Investors willingly speculated on mines and lost, except in a few instances. The rich mines, however, and their well-known dividends, attracted investors to other prospects in hopes of finding another bonanza. The incredible success of the Cripple Creek district, which boomed in the 1890s, caused many marginal districts to be opened in hopeful imitation. These districts were opened not because their ore was valuable, but because investors hoped that their ore would become valuable."

None of these mines could pay for its own excavation, so these moneyed folks from the Great Plains made a game of it, caught in the excitement of the elevated rhetoric flowing from the printing presses of newspapers from Colorado to New York. They hung on each blast through another wall of rock, certain that the next one would reveal the mother lode they had sought since 1859. In the Longs Peak district, however, mines produced nothing but low-grade gold, laced with copper veins that made the work harder, requiring "complicated metallurgy to remove the gold," Spude explained. "Special mills and smelters had been built in Colorado to handle these ores, but the expense of moving ore to mill caused a collapse of mining in Allenspark by the fall of 1896."

It should have been over then, allowing the farmers and ranchers who had abandoned their fields to pursue the too-good-to-be-true dream of a gold mine to return to their homes and begin to recoup their losses. The speculators had other ideas, however, and some of them went so far as to reopen the closed mines, spending far more than they could ever hope to make.

One such enterprise came to Colorado from Genoa, Nebraska, backed by Genoa bank president A. E. Green and Union Pacific Railroad engineer H. A. Riley. In 1898, the Genoa Mining Company bought some claims in Allenspark, near today's Meeker Park, and started digging. "The Genoa Mining Company is working right along," the *Longmont Ledger* reported on August 19, 1898. "They have free gold," meaning the gold that was easiest to mine, "and it looks as though they were going to strike the long lost rich vein of Longs Peak."

Green and Riley held out hope into 1899, when they constructed a shaft house, hired miners, and began to make plans to ship their bounty out of Colorado. Green told the media that the mine "was just a little flyer" but that it was turning out to be just as big a producer as the largest mines at Cripple Creek. He bragged that they had found "a streak of pyritic iron which assayed $200/ton." That was the last thing he said to the press, however, as any mention of the Genoa Mining Company vanished from public view before the year was out.

A larger Nebraskan operation, the Clara Belle Mining and Reduction Company, appeared in the area in 1901 and began opening up deserted mine shafts and building roads for the transport of ore. It bought up seventy claims, and its leadership boasted of a proprietary milling process that would reduce the cost of milling the ore to $1.50 per ton, an unheard-of possibility. This carefully guarded trade secret was the brainstorm of C. L. Tripp, a fairly well-known and experienced miner with decades of background in Colorado mining. Only he knew the secret, he said, and it was "too valuable to trust even to the protection of a patent right." It was based on "a chemical process which separates the refractory ores in vats and then readies the ore for simple amalgamation," he explained as cryptically as he could.

The company built an experimental mill, spending a whopping twenty thousand dollars to do so, but a year after construction and experimentation began, Tripp still had not produced a workable process. "By December 1902 the plant still was incomplete and the investors were tiring of Tripp's laboratory hocus pocus," Spude wrote. "Tripp was removed from the company, [and] he later organized the similarly ill-fated X-Ray Mining Company in nearby Nederland."

Clara Belle continued its operations, rebuilt the mill, and installed a tramway and a hydroelectric plant, and for a while it seemed that they might pull off a successful system. In the end, however, "the cost of reducing the ore was higher than the value of the mineral produced," Spude said. "After 1904, the company ceased operation."

The company's impact continued beyond its own corporate life, however. Other mining companies moved into the area around Allenspark, also opening mines that had shut down years before. For several years it looked as if the community might thrive on even this speculative mine business for the longer term, but by the end of the twentieth century's first decade, the mining operations had not achieved profitability, and the last ones shut down their shafts for the final time.

The time, backbreaking effort, and money spent in the attempt to get rich quick may seem like an enormous waste from a modern perspective, but one benefit remains: If the mines had paid out the hoped-for dividends, this area might have continued to be a massive mining operation today—and Rocky Mountain National Park might never have been created.

Frontier Hospitality

Estes Park has long ago become civilized, highly civilized, indeed fashionable. Hotels, private houses, guides, expeditions, and all the rest of it. But I would love to see again the place I knew so well in its primeval state. Spoilt, of course, it would appear to my eyes; but no work of man, except pits, mills, and factories, could destroy the grandeur, and the beauty, of Estes Park.
     —WINDHAM THOMAS WYNDHAM-QUIN
       EARL OF DUNRAVEN

MAKING THE DECISION TO BE AN UPSTANDING CITIZEN ON THE WEST-ern frontier in 1863 carried all kinds of perils, as Griffith J. Evans soon discovered. No sooner did he undertake a business venture in Colorado than his partner bilked him out of a small fortune, leaving Evans with no money and massive debt. The *Rocky Mountain News* delved into this years later, in 1874, when Evans would become not only famous but notorious, making a case for the man's character: "His sense of honesty compelled him to settle all claims against the firm, and not only his money, but his last team, went in this way."

Destitute and struggling to support his wife, Jane, and three children, Evans made do and somehow purchased the property Joel Estes had left behind in 1866. All they had to do was find a way to get their few belongings through the canyon—a twenty-mile journey—and up to Estes Park.

Jane Evans asked a friend, Captain George W. Brown, if he would be willing to help them. "As I had never visited the place, I offered to take them," Brown later related. "I had a good stout wagon and team doing nothing just then. My offer was enthusiastically accepted, so the following morning I went over to see what they would have to move in the way of household goods."

What he found tugged at his heart: a few sticks of furniture beyond repair, a broken stove, and a little bedding. "After loading these onto the wagon, I said, 'Now for the provisions.' Mrs. Evans said, 'We haven't any.'"

This was late fall; the Evans family intended to attempt to live off the land through a Colorado winter with not so much as a bag of flour to sustain them. Brown questioned them about their readiness to hunt and fish and discovered that they had a gun but no powder, so even deer hunting would be a monumental challenge.

"So we passed our camp and I divided my supplies with them, a sack of measly little potatoes and one of smutty flour, a little powder and lead and salt," Brown recalled. They made their way up the canyon to the Estes place, where one log house remained on the property, so the Evans family would have shelter at least, even if their furnishings had rattled apart in the wagon on the ride.

"We found quite a lot of cattle about the place, and succeeded in catching two young calves," Brown said. "By putting them in the corral over night we were able, after quite some difficulties, to get some milk from their mothers of the youngsters [*sic*] breakfast." The continued challenges would have overwhelmed less hardy individuals, as the captain noted: "Griff had to carry his saddles of venison on his shoulder from Estes to the John Reece place on the St. Vrain to trade for any further supplies, a walk of some forty miles or more. At that, he made good, making his home there for many years, or until his boys were nearly grown."

Evans's lot improved gradually over the next several years. When pioneer Abner Sprague and two schoolmates made their way into Estes Park for the first time, they came upon two men setting posts for a corral, and "what seemed to be a one-room log cabin, dirt-covered, a rough pine door and a small window on our side." The men turned out to be Griff Evans and James Nugent—the recluse known as Rocky Mountain Jim—who were just beginning to make changes to the Estes property.

Evans began raising cattle and bringing them to market, and he built several cabins alongside his own, outfitting them with all a traveler would need to be comfortable while enjoying the Rocky Mountain wilderness. He was one of the first to recognize the potential of the mountain air, glorious views, and robust recreation options as a draw in themselves, a reason for people of many stripes to travel into the western frontier for healing, adventure, and sport.

Through their own industry, Evans and his family set about making their property as attractive to tourists as they could. Isabella Bird landed there after her journey through the canyon (see the "Summits in Skirts" chapter), and she could not say enough about the comfort she enjoyed there:

> *I was hungry, and the air was frosty, and I was wondering what the prospects of food and shelter were in this enchanted region, when we came suddenly upon a small lake, close to which was a very trim-looking log cabin, with a flat mud roof, with four smaller ones; picturesquely dotted about near it, two corrals, a long shed, in front of which a steer was being killed, a log dairy with a water wheel, some hay piles, and various evidences of comfort; and two men, on serviceable horses, were just bringing in some tolerable cows to be milked. A short, pleasant-looking man ran up to me and shook hands gleefully . . . I recognized in him a countryman, and he introduced himself as Griffith Evans, a Welshman from the slate quarries near Llanberis. When the cabin door was opened I saw a good-sized log room, unchinked, however, with windows of infamous glass, looking two ways; a rough stone fireplace, in which pine longs, half as large as I am, were burning; a boarded floor, a round table, two rocking chairs, a carpet-covered backwoods couch; and skins, Indian bows and arrows, wampum belts, and antlers, fitly decorated the rough walls. . . . So in this glorious upper world, with the mountain pines behind and the clear lake in front, in the "blue hollow at the foot of Long's Peak," at a height of 7,500 feet, where the hoar frost crisps the grass every night of the year, I have found far more than I ever dared to hope for.*

When Sprague and a group of friends passed through again in 1872, Sprague noted, "We spent the last evening at the Evans home, and we enjoyed it as much as any evening in the park. Mr. Evans was a Welshman who entertained us with Welsh songs, which he rendered in good shape, and we all joined in singing the songs of the day. We also danced the now out-of-date dances." Two or three other guests had stopped there as well, and Sprague now called the property a "ranch," acknowledging its expansion.

Evans often receives credit as the first to bring the dude ranch, a form of vacation or extended stay that has its origins in northern Colorado, to Estes Park. Expedition companies, leading city dwellers from the eastern states or wealthy Europeans looking for "sport," began in the late 1860s to construct lodges and hunting camps in areas where hunting and fishing were plentiful. The lodges served as comfortable places for other family members to stay while guests hunted, providing alternative recreation options for spouses and children. Some offered a range of sleeping accommodations as well, with tent camping for people who wanted a truly "western" experience, as well as cabins for people who preferred privacy at the end of the day.

The Evans ranch remained the only option for accommodations in Estes Park for several years, until a different kind of proprietor arrived in the area—one with more money than the Evans family could ever hope to accumulate and nothing to do but spend it on his own whims.

THE ENGLISH COMPANY

Windham Thomas Wyndham-Quin, fourth Earl of Dunraven and Mount-Earl in Ireland, first visited the American West as a sportsman in 1871. Traveling to hunt big game served as an exciting pastime for the wealthy throughout Europe in the 1870s—and today, for that matter—so when Lord Dunraven heard of the opportunities to hunt buffalo and elk (what the English called "wapiti") on the Great Plains and beyond, he made the ocean voyage and took the new cross-continental railroad from New York to Nebraska, engaging the famous Texas Jack Omohundro and Buffalo Bill Cody as his guides.

He had such a good time that he returned in 1872, and he, his entourage, and his guides traversed the Nebraska plains and headed out to Wyoming, no doubt bagging themselves some sizable animal trophies.

Windham Thomas
Wyndham-Quin,
Earl of Dunraven
DENVER PUBLIC LIBRARY

On the way back east, he stopped in Denver just in time for Christmas, and befriended Theodore Whyte, a Devonshire, England, native who had lived in Colorado since the 1860s. Whyte told Dunraven tales of wonderful hunting not far away in Estes Park. Right after the holiday, Dunraven and several friends bought horses and a mule, packed "some necessaries," and made their way through the bitter cold to the remote Rocky Mountain valley.

Dunraven found himself smitten. "Estes Park was, and still must be, a glorious place," he wrote in his memoir, *Past Times and Pastimes*, in 1922. "A great plain, or rather park, for a huge well-timbered park best describes it, intersected by numerous streams, branches of the Great

The Earl of Dunraven built this sprawling home on his land in Estes Park.
DENVER PUBLIC LIBRARY

Thompson, opening into great, glorious, heavily timbered valleys and cañons, the whole dominated by snow-clad Pikes Peak. There was no track in those days; and it was a paradise for the hunter and trapper. Mountain sheep, black-tail and white-tail deer in abundance, and an occasional mountain lion or bear."

The only inhabitants he met were Evans, a countryman from Wales "who made a living I don't know how," and Mountain Jim, "who trapped—an extraordinary character, civil enough when sober, but when drunk, which was as often as he could manage, violent and abusive, and given to declamation in Greek and Latin."

Dunraven returned the following year, and the year after that, and developed so great and immediate a passion for Estes Park that he decided that he would remain there, acquire as much of it as possible for his own, and turn it into a private game preserve for himself and his friends. "Cattle could feed all winter, for the snow never lay," he wrote. "It was an ideal cattle-ranch, and to that purpose we put it. . . . We pre-empted, and bought land along the water, and, commanding the water, had a great area of splendid grazing country, and we put in cattle."

Dunraven formed an entity called Estes Park Company, Ltd., or the "English Company" to locals, hired some Denver lawyers and met some city bankers, and had the whole of Estes Park surveyed professionally. He then used the Homestead Act of 1862 against itself, convincing individuals in Front Range towns to put down shallow roots by claiming 160 acres of land each and immediately selling it to him. It was easy money, and more than thirty-five men agreed to the scheme. He chose his acreage carefully, including streams that led out of the valley, so that he paid for 8,000 acres but actually held control of nearly 15,000 acres. The complicit homesteaders made about five dollars per acre.

"A new Company, of which the Earl of Dunraven is the principal stockholder, has purchased all the available lands in Estes Park, embracing some 6,000 acres," the *Greeley Tribune* reported in August 1874. "The Company proposes making extensive and costly improvements. Among these will be a large hotel, saw mill, new roads through the park, a hotel at Longmont, and a half way house on the road between that place and the park."

The *Denver Tribune* and the *Fort Collins Standard* freely expressed outrage about the deal. "We are informed from reliable sources that one of the most villainous land steals ever perpetrated in Colorado has been enacted in Estes Park within the last few months, by some Englishmen, who through the perjury of various parties, have succeeded in gaining possession of some 6,000 acres of land lying on either side of, and controlling the different streams in the Park. We expect to be able to give the particulars of this swindle next week." It took the *Standard* two weeks to collect enough information to run another short piece on August 26: "We have been unable to get as full particulars as was expected, yet it has been ascertained that a large lot of land, aggregating 4,960 acres, has been proved up without settlement, and the returns sent to Washington for patents. It also transpires that the greater portion of this land was filed on in February and proved up in May, a little irregularity which the ex-officials of the land office at Denver may be able to explain."

This somewhat illuminating investigative reporting continued: "Attorney General Alleman's attention has been called to this business, and he sends us word that if we will send a man to Denver to investigate, and lay the whole thing before him, he will write to Washington and have the patents withheld." It concludes, "We most respectfully decline to attend to the Attorney General's business."

Regardless of the *Standard*'s unwillingness to aid in the investigation, legal battles began and went on for years. "It became evident that we were not to be left monarchs of all we surveyed," Dunraven wrote in his book. "Folks were drifting in prospecting, fossicking, pre-empting, making claims; so we prepared for civilisation."

In 1877, after losing all nearly half of his holdings in lawsuits, Dunraven bought a sawmill in San Francisco and had it shipped into Estes Park, and he used the milled wood to build the Estes Park Hotel—or the English Hotel, as the locals called it. He "did pretty well with a Chinese cook who could make venison and anything else out of bogged cow beef," he said. The three-story hotel, the first of its kind in the area, had a columned porch the entire length of the front of the building, and the porch roof served as a second-floor deck, giving guests wide views of the surrounding scenery. The story goes that Albert Bierstadt, one of the West's most celebrated artists, helped Dunraven choose the location of this hotel to maximize the impact of the landscape from the veranda and every window.

Dunraven kept the property for thirty years, returning annually in the late 1870s and early 1880s and bringing many of the English nobility to enjoy the area's hunting, but he faced so many challenges to his ownership that he finally relinquished it. "People came in disputing claims, kicking up rows," he said. "Exorbitant land taxes got into arrears; we were in constant litigation. The show could not be managed from home, and we were in danger of being frozen out."

In the interim, Dunraven had poured nearly three hundred thousand dollars into construction and improvements, according to the *Denver Post* in April 1905. He had built a lavish estate that the newspaper called "one of the finest summer homes in Colorado," complete with its own chapel (which had burned down earlier in 1905).

Bits of news that Lord Dunraven might finally be ready to sell began appearing in local papers in 1903. An item in several newspapers in

The Stanley Hotel, built on land once owned by the Earl of Dunraven, remains one of the most popular hotels in Estes Park. CAROL HIGHSMITH, NATIONAL PARK SERVICE

April 1903 reported that "a syndicate of Denver and Boston capitalists has purchased 11,000 acres of land in Estes Park, together with about 30,000 acres of range lands, comprising the former holdings of the Earl of Dunraven and of the Estes Park Land and Improvement Company. It is proposed to build a hotel and sanatorium, and also to conduct a large general store."

Newspapers throughout Colorado reported in October 1905, "The 7,000 acre ranch of the Earl of Dunraven in Estes Park has been purchased by Miller Porter of Denver, together with the hotel, cottages and livestock on the place. The price is said to be $100,000," although some sources suggest it was as low as $80,000, representing a significant loss for the Irish nobleman. "Miller Porter" is not identified any further, but it may have been a business entity or law firm representing two eager buyers: B. D. Sanborn, owner of the Estes Park Development Company, and Freelan Oscar Stanley, who bought half of Sanborn's interest. These developers were ready to move ahead with improvements that would further Estes Park's reputation as a resort area. Stanley carried on the legacy of hospitality and built the now-famous, eighty-eight room Stanley Hotel (the inspiration for Stephen King's novel *The Shining*), and the first modern road to Estes Park, over which he could drive his own

Other properties that are now part of Rocky Mountain National Park include the McGraw Ranch, which served as a guest ranch for more than sixty years.
LIBRARY OF CONGRESS

invention, the Stanley Steamer steam-powered automobile, to and from more populated areas.

When the earl finally agreed to relinquish control of some of his Estes Park property, the Estes Park Development company began the process of updating the English Hotel with a complete remodel and refurnishing, and converting the Dunraven summer home into a country club. The new developer intended to improve transportation facilities and spend a great deal of money on advertising materials, ushering in a new era for Estes Park as a tourist destination.

"The development of the place has always been retarded because of the refusal of the Earl of Dunraven to let the control pass out of his hands," the *Denver Post* said. "A few months ago a deal was completed

Estes Park continued to grow despite Dunraven's hold on much of the land until 1907. LIBRARY OF CONGRESS

by Mr. La Coste in London which placed the control into the hands of the new organization."

Dunraven's aging English Hotel, an all-wooden structure, went up in flames in 1911, a loss that cleared the way for more development of Estes Park's still-burgeoning hospitality industry.

Dunraven had only this to say, some years later in *Past Times and Pastimes*: "We sold for what we could get and cleared out, and I have never been there since."

The Killing of Mountain Jim

It would seem that an all-wise Providence has spared my life; that a hell-born plot to deprive a man of his life might be exposed. Justice is sometimes tardy, and the red-handed assassin and highway murderer oftentimes escape the gallows and the prison cell. Sometimes by successful escape; sometimes by resort to gold. Men in official position as protectors of the people prostituting their sacred trusts. Private citizens throwing so much perjury into the scales for a stipulated price, depriving an innocent part of his life or liberty, and all for gold.

—James Nugent
The Standard, Fort Collins, Colo., August 12, 1874

No discussion of these early days in Estes Park can be complete without a review of the last days in the life of Rocky Mountain Jim, the notorious recluse with the erudite manner who alternately charmed and terrified visitors.

"There was a time in the early history of Colorado when human blood letting seemed to be almost a fine art," wrote Ansel Watrous in the *Estes Park Trail* in 1922. "That was before Colorado had been organized as a Territory, and when the population was made up largely of gold hunters, adventurers and desperadoes who counted human life as but little value. Often a word and the crack of a gun gave notice that another victim of the lust for blood had bitten the dust, and sometimes the crack of the gun came first."

Estes Park and its surrounding open land stood in the heart of the Old West, a place where everyone carried a weapon and gunfights could erupt in seconds. "Every man was a law unto himself, and the destroyer of human life stood a better chance of saving his neck than did a horse thief," Watrous observed.

There were laws, of course, and courts to see that the perpetrators were brought to justice, but in small towns on the edges of wilderness areas, conventional law enforcement had not yet taken hold. So in 1874, when the relationship between Jim Nugent and Griff Evans deteriorated, people around them knew that a confrontation could happen at any time—and such a clash could easily end in death.

What prompted the bad blood between them? Some, including the Earl of Dunraven, said it was about a girl. "Evans and Jim had a feud, as per usual about a woman—Evans' daughter," Dunraven wrote. He could have been sloughing off a darker rivalry, however, one that included the earl himself.

Betty Freudenburg, author of *Facing the Frontier: The Story of the MacGregor Ranch*, noted that the relationship between Evans and Nugent went sour when the two men had "differing opinions on the earl's land acquisition plans. . . . The most likely reason for the killing was Dunraven's wish to get rid of the valley's hostile gatekeeper, who had been said to have taken pot shots at trespassers." She acknowledges that Nugent's designs on Evans's daughter may have thrown gasoline on the flames, and "the fire of their antagonisms may have been stoked by liquor."

Dunraven recalled the event from his perspective, protected out of the line of fire in Evans's lodge. "One fine day I was sitting by the fire, and Evans asleep on a sort of sofa, when some one rushed in shouting, 'Get up; here's Mountain Jim in the coral [*sic*], and his is looking very ugly.' Up jumped Evans, grabbed a shot gun, and went out."

Even though he wrote his account of the event in 1922, Dunraven may have felt the need to set down his own record of what he witnessed and why. He knew all too well that Nugent bitterly opposed Dunraven's land grab activities, especially because Nugent controlled some of the land that the wealthy Irishman hoped to acquire. "His cabin sat at the head of Muggins Gulch, dominating the main entrance to Estes Park," wrote historian Kathy Weiser-Alexander in a 2018 account of the events of June 19, 1874. As Evans had chosen to cooperate with Dunraven and sell him his own land, Nugent had a significant bone to pick with his former ally.

Reverend Elkanah Lamb, a pillar of the Estes Park community with a residence at the base of Longs Peak, spoke out repeatedly against the earl's land deal and the trouble the nobleman had brought to them. He declared that Nugent had "declined to permit this fraternity of English snobs and aristocrats to pass through his sacred precincts any more, there being at the time no other way in or out of the Park."

Some in the community willingly accepted the former explanation, however, that Jim had taken a liking to Evans's daughter, who was seventeen, a situation Evans could not tolerate. When Dunraven brought in a young Englishman named William Haigh to see to his affairs in Estes Park, Evans's daughter chose this new man as the object of her affections. "They were often seen riding together," Watrous noted, "which stirred 'Mountain Jim's' anger toward Evans to the very depths."

On June 10, according to one account, Nugent ambushed Evans with the intent to kill him, firing his gun at him and missing. This botched effort to eliminate the rancher only infuriated Jim more, and nine days later, on June 19, he arrived at Evans's home "in a frightful mood, threatening to kill Evans and Haigh if they dared to come out in the open."

Nugent himself told the story entirely differently, in a letter published in the August 12, 1874, issue of the *Fort Collins Standard*:

> *On the nineteenth day of [June] while riding peaceably along a highway in company with one William Brown, when near the residence of one Griffith Evans, he approached me with a double-barreled shot gun in his hands, and when within a few steps, without warning, raised his gun and fired, killing the horse I was riding and inflicting a wound upon my person which fell me to the earth, and after I had fallen he deliberately walked up and shot me again through the head, turned upon his heel and disappeared in his house without even the enquiry whether I was dead. Immediately the press teems with report that Rocky Mountain Jim, a desperado of Estes Park, while attempting to take the life of one, Evans, was shot so that if not dead, will die. Served him right, &c.*

While I lay for weeks suffering a hundred deaths from the wounds inflicted by the hand of this would-be assassin, and his cowardly coadjutor, Haigh, who had hundreds of times threatened my life, and while the tragedy was being enacted slunk into Evans' cabin, and finally wanted to empty the contents of his brave English pistols into me when I was pronounced dead. Evans then flies to a justice of the peace, pleads guilty to assault and battery with intent to kill, and is bound over to the district court.

Shots were indeed fired—quite a lot of them, in fact, though it's not clear whether Nugent fired back at any point, and no one else on the scene took a bullet. Several of the shots ended up in Nugent's skull. "He was not dead, but refused to be carried into Evans' house," Dunraven wrote. "We carried him down to the creek, and fixed him up as well as we could, and he made a solemn declaration, as a man who would presently be before his Maker, that he had not begun the scrap, and that it was sheer murder. However, he did not go before his Maker, and after a while we got him back to his shanty."

A doctor came and examined Nugent, and concluded that he would die very soon, "for he had one bullet in his skull and his brains were oozing out," Dunraven said.

Nugent, with what he thought might be his dying breath, accused Griff Evans of firing the fatal shot, and it seemed likely that he would know who he saw aim at him and pull the trigger. No one refuted this claim, so law enforcement followed through and arrested Evans, brought him to Fort Collins for a preliminary hearing, and charged him with assault with a deadly weapon with intent to kill. Dunraven said Evans was "at once liberated on nominal bail"—a sum one article said was $1,500 and another claimed was $2,500 (either of which Evans was unlikely to feel was nominal).

But Jim survived, though he could not truly hope to recover with such significant injuries to his head and no modern medicine to remove the bullets or repair his wounds. Several weeks later the doctor had him brought into town and made him comfortable at a hotel, where he received what medical treatment could be offered. In the interim, Nugent did what he could to set the record straight. He continued in his letter to the *Standard*:

> *On the 14th ult., when the court sat at Fort Collins, and while I was still lying between life and death, the prosecuting attorney, without even coming to see me, although I had been lying within one mile of his residence for days, without hearing my story, goes before the grand jury and tries to have me indicted for assault with intent to kill, and who are the witnesses? Why Evans, the would-be assassin, and his accessory, Haigh. . . . Haigh swore he was sitting in Evans' door, saw James Nugent and Brown coming down the road, he got up, went into the house where Evans was lying on the bed and said "Evans, Rocky Mountain Jim is coming, you will not see me shot down like a dog, will you?"*

After this letter ran in the paper, the court swore out a warrant for Haigh's arrest as an accessory to the shooting and moved quickly to schedule a trial for Saturday, August 30. In the days before the trial, an unnamed editor of the *Denver Tribune* took it upon himself to meet Haigh face-to-face and interview him about his ongoing conflicts with Mountain Jim. "As between Evans and Jim we have nothing to say, but we *know* Mr. Haigh to be all that he assumes—a traveling English gentleman of wealth and leisure, and the last person in the world to seek or create unnecessary trouble. We sincerely trust his annoyances may not disgust him with our territory, as he belongs to a class of men that are an honor to any community, even though they be devoid of the rank and wealth that Mr. Haigh enjoys."

With such an editorial in the local paper and rerun by the *Fort Collins Standard* on August 26, the media all but dared the court to find fault with the genteel William Haigh. In this atmosphere of acceptance and even relief at Mountain Jim's incapacitation, the district court brought Haigh and Evans to a brief and hasty trial.

Haigh had to answer to just one charge. "The only ground of complaint against Mr. Haigh was that when Mr. Evans had shot Jim the first time he (Mr. Haigh) said, 'Give him the other barrel,'" the *Standard* reported.

The trial of Griffith Evans for the murder of Jim Nugent took place at the Larimer County Courthouse, in Fort Collins. DENVER PUBLIC LIBRARY

"His reasons for desiring Evans to give Jim the benefit of the other barrel were very good, inasmuch as Jim had threatened his life on divers [*sic*] occasions, and at one time punched him in the face and eyes with a rifle at full cock, and had used every endeavor to drive him from the park." The reporter went on to say that after such a pummeling, it was "only natural" that Haigh would want Evans to shoot Jim dead, and that the man's death would be "a benefit, if not to Jim, to the rest of the community."

"Haigh is as free as the wind, neither one of them are under a dollar of bond," Nugent wrote in fury even before he heard of this verdict. "I, a law-abiding American citizen, have been shot down by two English ruffians who boast of royal 'blood' coursing through their veins, and well-filled pockets which they are willing to empty into the lap of the man who can keep them from Canyon City by prostituting official capacity. . . . Great God! Is this your boasted Colorado?"

Testimony also revealed that Jim often rushed into Evans's home "brandishing a cocked revolver." This behavior drove Evans to distraction, the paper continued, and he "concluded to put a stop to it, which he did in a very effectual manner."

In light of these stories of antagonism on Nugent's part, the judge found both Haigh and Evans not guilty. "The only blame which can be attached to Mr. Evans is that he did not give Jim the deserved dose long ago," the report finished.

Jim finally passed away on September 7 at the Collins House in the midafternoon. The newspaper offered this journalistically objective obituary: "Mountain Jim is an old mountaineer, having come to Colorado, or what was then Kansas, in 1854, since which time he has gained a livelihood by hunting and trapping. When sober, he was peaceable and well disposed toward all, but when under the influence of liquor was vindictive, overbearing and given to domineering over everybody against whom he held a grudge. Of late years he has been addicted to hard drinking, and consequently made himself very obnoxious to all of his supposed enemies, which course finally culminated in his being shot by Mr. Evans. Whether he died from his wounds or not will be determined by the verdict of the coroner's jury."

Years later, Dunraven took the opportunity to have a last word: "The case was eventually tried, with the result of a verdict to the effect that Evans was quite justified, and that it was a pity he had not done it sooner."

There's another legend connected with Nugent's death, and it involves the remarkable Isabella Bird, with whom Jim had spent considerable time in the fall and winter of 1873. As he left her at the Greeley stage station on the day she departed Colorado, Jim met an English dandy whom Isabella calls "Mr. Fodder," who happened to be on the stage wagon. She had met this fop earlier in her trip, so he greeted her warmly and then made Nugent's acquaintance for the first time. "He was now dressed in the extreme of English dandyism, and when I introduced them, he put out a small hand cased in a perfectly-fitting lemon-colored kid glove," she said. She then provided this footnote: "This was a truly unfortunate introduction. It was the first link in the chain of circumstances which brought about Mr. Nugent's untimely end, and it was at this person's instigation (when overcome by fear) that Evans fired the shot which proved fatal."

Who was Mr. Fodder, and how was he involved? Historians, novelists, and hopeless romantics have worked to fit these pieces together for a century and a half, but some questions must be left unanswered. Should you visit Fort Collins, however, stop at Grandview Cemetery and visit Rocky Mountain Jim's final resting place in an unmarked grave, and perhaps, just this once, a dead man will tell a tale.

Forever Preserved: Enos Mills and the Creation of a National Park

A National Park is a fountain of life. It is a matchless potential factor for good in national life. It holds within its magic realm benefits that are health-giving, educational, economic, that further efficiency and ethical relations, and are inspirational. Everyone needs to play, and to play out of doors. Without parks and outdoor life all that is best in civilization will be smothered. To save ourselves, to prevent our perishing, to enable us to live at our best and happiest, parks are necessary. Within National parks is room—glorious room—room in which to find ourselves, in which to think and hope, to dream and plan, to rest and resolve.

—ENOS A. MILLS

SOME OF US CAN POINT TO THE MOMENT IN WHICH EVERYTHING IN OUR lives changed, when we moved from exploring our options or gliding aimlessly through our days to a focus on a single path—a passion-driven trajectory. For nineteen-year-old Enos Mills, it was a chance meeting on a beach in San Francisco, when he happened to cross paths with a man fascinating a small group of people with his knowledge of the local plant life.

"As soon as these people scattered I asked him concerning a long-rooted plant that someone had dug from a sand dune," Mills wrote years later. "The man was John Muir and he proceeded to describe the manners, customs and adventures of this plant, one of the yuccas. . . . Then he

Enos A. Mills is considered the father of Rocky Mountain National Park.
NATIONAL PARK SERVICE

invited me for a four mile walk across the sand hills and through Golden Gate Park to the end of the car line. During this walk he incited me to do many things, some of which I fear will not be done by the time I reach three score and ten."

John Muir, of course, was the nation's most impassioned proponent of wilderness preservation at the time, an author and activist whose work had led to the federal protection of Yosemite and Sequoia National Parks long before the National Park Service was formed. Mills already had a well-honed appreciation of open spaces and the outdoors, but Muir took the embers of this fire and built them into a blaze. He encouraged the young man to travel and see all of the nation's grandest natural places, and Mills spent the next six months traversing the Pacific coast, seeing the Sequoia redwood forests, Muir's beloved Yosemite—named a national park the previous year by President Benjamin Harrison—and Death

Valley, lands as different from one another as water and coffee, yet each with its extraordinary natural wonders.

"He came to believe, as preached his elder master, that outdoor recreation was not merely a luxury, but a necessity," wrote Patricia Fazio in her lengthy master's degree thesis at the University of Wyoming, in which she explored the process Mills pursued to protect Colorado's Front Range and surrounding lands as a national park. "This, he felt, was the 'ideal recreation,' promoting health, education, and efficiency."

At the time of this chance meeting, just four national parks existed in the United States: Yellowstone, General Grant (which would become Kings Canyon), Sequoia, and Yosemite. The US Congress named others over the course of the next two decades: Mount Rainier in the state of Washington, Crater Lake in Oregon, Wind Cave in South Dakota, Petrified Forest in Arizona, Mesa Verde in Colorado, and Glacier in northwestern Montana, but the formation of an administrative body to look after these parks would not take place until 1916, when President Woodrow Wilson signed the bill creating the National Park Service. With that bill would come established processes to make a clear case for an area's preservation, to plan its management and budget, and to bring this information before a congressional committee to have it considered in the House and Senate. But when Mills began his own efforts to protect this corner of the Rockies, he could only reference grassroots efforts, some of which had failed miserably. He needed to bushwhack his own trail through the dense political forest to have any hope of protecting his beloved park forever.

THE LURE OF THE PEAK

Enos Abijah Mills arrived in Estes Park in the summer of 1884, a fourteen-year-old boy with a strange digestive condition that had rendered him slight and skinny. His parents had left their native Kansas and spent the summer of 1859 prospecting for gold in the Colorado wilderness eleven years before he was born, but his mother told him many tales of the clear mountain air, sunshine, high peaks, and open spaces, and he came to believe that there might be healing for him in this spectacular part of the country. His father may have been just as happy to see him go, as his son's ailment prohibited him from doing chores on the family farm, an issue his father called his "stubborn streak."

Enos picked up odd jobs in Estes Park and did indeed become stronger, buoyed by the extraordinary landscape around him and the views of Longs Peak. He heard about people climbing the mountain, something that had become fairly commonplace by that time. Young Mills befriended Reverend Elkanah Lamb, who owned a ranch in Longs Peak Valley, about seven miles south of Estes Park. Lamb had become the first regular guide for Longs Peak climbers, and he provided parties with accommodations at his ranch before and after their climb. His son, Carlyle, had taken over the guiding responsibilities by the time Mills hired on at the ranch, and he and the guests entertained Enos with stories of the mountain's rigors, its perils, and its rapturous views as he did his chores and tended to the livestock.

One day Enos convinced Carlyle to allow him to accompany a climbing party. That first climb changed his life, and in 1887 he made his first solo climb to the summit. After that he strove to become a guide in his own right, learning the ins and outs of the various routes and the effects of climbing from 9,000 to 14,259 feet on visitors not acclimated to a full mile's difference in altitude. "'Feeling the altitude' would often be more correctly expressed as feeling the effects of high living!" he said in his essay, "Going to the Top." "True, climbing high into a brighter, finer atmosphere diminishes the elastic clasp—the pressure of the air—and causes physiological changes. These usually are beneficial. . . . In the overwhelming number of cases the lowland visitor is permanently benefited by a visit to the mountains and especially by a climb in the heights."

In 1889, Mills became a guide, and over the course of several summers he climbed Longs Peak no less than 257 times and led thousands of people up the mountain. In his years living at the base of Longs Peak, he staked a claim and built himself a cabin on a plot of land suggested by Reverend Lamb, just across a stream from the Lamb ranch with a view of the mountain from his front window. Here he had the privacy he needed to study, as he had left school behind when he set out from Kansas, so he delved into grammar, history, and arithmetic, and improving his own writing skills—a skill set that would serve him well for the rest of his life. He also studied the world around him, learning the names of plants and animals and their natural history, to better understand their life cycles, their interdependence, and their roles within the greater environment.

In the off-seasons, Mills sought mining work in Butte, Montana, and quickly worked his way up through the ranks from nipper (essentially an underground errand boy) to engineer, using the money he made to feed his travel habit. When not hard at work underground, he made copious use of Butte's library and read all of the great thinkers of the day, building his own understanding of the natural world as well as his comprehension of the national economy, the workings of politics, and the nation's history. A chance meeting with a doctor from New York changed his life as well: Mills's often debilitating digestive complaint finally received a well-informed diagnosis, as the physician determined that Mills had a sensitivity to starches (perhaps what we now know as celiac disease). Removing these foods from his diet changed the young man's life, making him more able to pursue his love of the outdoors than ever before.

When the Butte mine closed as the result of a fire disaster in the fall of 1889, Mills took advantage of his free time and traveled to San Francisco, where his encounter with John Muir coalesced his love of natural places with his enlightened perspective. After six months of traveling through California and seeing all of its wonders, he settled into business school in San Francisco, gaining the skills he would need to take an office position with the mine at the beginning of 1891. Perhaps it comes as no surprise that Mills found himself ill-suited for long, stationary days in an office setting—after just a few weeks, he gave notice, packed up a bedroll and a few necessities, and set out on foot to Yellowstone National Park to see what the nation's first protected wilderness was like.

Mills spent the winter and spring at Yellowstone, making the most of this opportunity to explore. In his wanderings he met US Army Corps of Engineers general Hiram M. Chittenden, one of the leaders in developing Yellowstone for public access, planning roads and trails and other required facilities. Once again, Mills seized the opportunity to spend time with a man who shared his own passion for magnificent

Making Rocky Mountain a national park would foster construction of more trails to remote areas. CAROL HIGHSMITH, NATIONAL PARK SERVICE

open spaces, especially one intimately familiar with park planning. That summer, as Mills joins a US Geological Survey team and remained in the park for several more months, he recognized many similarities between Yellowstone and his beloved Rocky Mountains. He started to consider the germ of an idea: permanent federal preservation of an area that remained, in his mind, one of the most spectacular in any part of the country that he had seen so far.

The Forces against Preservation

Let's take a moment to get up to speed with the political and economic environment of the 1890s and early 1900s, so we can understand the challenges facing the survival of the forests, plains, waterways, and unusual natural features of the American West.

In March 1891, the Forest Reserve Act—not a bill in itself, but part of a much larger bill about public lands—gave the President the power to "set apart and reserve" any forests on public land as "public reservations." The President at the time was Benjamin Harrison, and he moved quickly to create fifteen reserves, protecting more than thirteen million acres of forests and waterways.

As you might imagine, this created immediate controversy. What were these lands set aside for? Were they parks that must be kept pristine and free from human commerce or interference, or were they open to logging for commercial use? The Forest Reserve Act became the first definitive effort to address what settlers across the country had begun to see as more and more people arrived in what had been open, untouched wilderness. "Giving people easy access to timber, wildlife, water, and other resources in the public domain came to be questioned," wrote C. W. Buchholtz in his book, *Rocky Mountain National Park: A History*. "Laws regulating the use of public lands had to be refined. Many practices common to frontier life were now defined as abuses. People realized that lumbermen stole timber from land they never owned; forests had been recklessly cut from Maine to California; reforestation hardly existed; stockmen ruined the range, herding too many cattle upon it; rampant logging brought erosion and flooding; forest fires raged unchecked; miners dumped tailings helter-skelter. Following an era of exploitation, a few people reacted, perhaps as a national conscience, expressing concern for the future of the land."

After considerable disagreement, even within a formal commission set up to come to a useful conclusion, Congress passed the Forest Management Act in 1897. This act clarified that forest reserves were meant

With logging operations denuding sections of the Rocky Mountain landscape, Mills sought to protect the area as a national park. LIBRARY OF CONGRESS

"to furnish a continuous supply of timber for the use and necessities of citizens of the United States."

Environmentalists, including John Muir, saw this as an affront to their efforts to protect some areas as national parks. By this time, Muir had become president of the Sierra Club, which formed in 1892 in the midst of this controversy to serve the dual purpose of making the Pacific Coast's mountain regions open to the public, and to "enlist the support and cooperation of the people and the government in preserving the forests and other natural features of the Sierra Nevada Mountains." The Sierra Club became a staunch advocacy group for the newly created Yosemite National Park, Sequoia National Park, and General Grant National Park (Kings Canyon), and it served as a model for other activists who saw the value in creating such organizations in their own regions.

Meanwhile, naming the nation's first national parks had done little to actually protect them. No one in the federal government had the express responsibility of maintaining these lands, so the parks languished, and those who came to explore them were essentially free to do whatever they chose within their boundaries. While the War Department had dispatched US Cavalry officers to keep the riffraff out and to discourage poaching and other misuse of the resources within the parks, that was as far as the department's oversight went.

As Congress created Mount Rainier National Park in 1899, under President William McKinley, and President Theodore Roosevelt signed Crater Lake and Wind Cave National Parks into law, the management of some of these new properties fell to the Department of Agriculture and some to the Department of the Interior. No one headed up an office of park management, however, as no such office had been created, and no rules of governance or management had been set down by any administrative body. Several congressional representatives attempted to rectify the issue by introducing legislation to form an office of national park management, but these bills met with criticism, opposition, and literally years of revision in committees.

One bill did find its way into law, largely because it received the personal attention of Teddy Roosevelt. The Antiquities Act, which Roosevelt signed into law on June 8, 1906, came to pass because of the urgent need to protect Chaco Canyon, one of the most extensive sets of Native American Puebloan ruins in the United States, from artifact hunters who picked through the ruins indiscriminately and gathered clay pots and other relics for their personal collections. Roosevelt sent Iowa congressman John F. Lacey, who had authored one of the bills to create a national park oversight office, and anthropologist Edgar Lee Hewett, to survey Chaco Canyon and determine the extent of the damage to date. The report they presented moved Congress to act, giving the president the power to create national monuments to protect "historic landmarks, historic and prehistoric structures, and other objects of historic or scientific interest that are situated upon the lands owned or controlled by the Government of the United States." Roosevelt gleefully used this to protect a total of eighteen sites, including many natural landmarks and manmade antiquities throughout the West: Devil's Tower in Wyoming; Grand Canyon and Petrified Forest in Arizona; Cinder Cone, Lassen

Peak, Pinnacles, and Muir Woods in California; El Morro in New Mexico; Jewel Cave in South Dakota; Natural Bridges in Utah; Lewis and Clark Cavern in Montana; Wheeler Geologic Area in Colorado and Mount Olympus in Washington; and Native American ruins including Montezuma Castle, Tonto, and Tumacacori in Arizona; and Chaco Culture and Gila Cliff Dwellings in New Mexico.

All of these sites required management, and soon the need for a central bureau to oversee parks and monuments became critical. "Rather than entrusting national monuments to one agency, Congress had left each under care of the bureau administering the land," noted Fazio in her thesis. By 1911, this had resulted in uneven oversight, bureaucratic headaches, and rivalries between the US Forest Service, which had responsibility for thirteen monuments, and the Interior Department, which had responsibility for fifteen.

The first draft of the bill to create a "Bureau of National Parks" came from the desk of Secretary of the Interior Richard A. Ballinger during William Howard Taft's presidency. It fell to Ballinger to resolve the struggles between departments by creating a separate silo for the parks and monuments. He confessed to Taft in his annual report that "the volume and importance of the work of the supervision of the national parks and reserves under the Secretary of the Interior has passed beyond the stage of satisfactory control by operations carried on with the small force available in the Secretary's office."

Ballinger and the members of the American Civic Association—including Frederick Law Olmsted Jr., son of the most famous and respected landscape architect of his generation—drafted, redrafted, revised, and finalized a bill, and later that year Senator Reed Smoot of Utah introduced it in Congress. Its path to passage met with a series of perils, including foresting advocates who did not approve of protection for forests that did not include the option of harvest by logging. Some objected to adding another layer of bureaucracy, protesting that the government was already too large and expensive to run. Five years of obstacles, further revisions, and countermeasures finally came to a satisfactory result: "An Act to Establish a National Park Service, and for Other Purposes" passed in Congress on August 25, 1916. The new office under the Department of the Interior would "promote and regulate the use of the Federal areas known as national parks, monuments, and reservations . . . which purpose is to conserve the scenery and the natural and historic objects and the wild life therein and to provide for the enjoyment of the same in such manner and by such means as will leave them unimpaired for the enjoyment of future generations."

Ten years before the National Park Service was signed into law, however, Enos Mills waded into this miasma of political turmoil, his work to create Rocky Mountain National Park beginning even before the Antiquities Act could have provided an avenue toward permanent preservation.

ROCKY MOUNTAIN IN PERIL

By 1905, when the germ of an idea started to sprout, Mills had taken ownership of Reverend Lamb's lodge at the base of Longs Peak. His reputation as an expert on the region and as a dedicated outdoorsman led to an unusual state appointment: He became the "state snow inspector," which meant that he spent the winter hiking through the Rocky Mountains and taking measurements of the snow's depth and moisture level at various elevations.

In between these solitary treks on snowshoes into some of the highest and most remote areas in Colorado, he used his now-solid skills as a writer and public speaker to advocate for the preservation of forests, mountains, and other natural features in the state's most glorious scenic areas, land that could just as easily be developed to death.

"I never see a little tree bursting from the earth, peeping confidently up among the withered leaves, without wondering how long it will live or what trials or triumphs it will have," he wrote in his book, *Wild Life on the Rockies.*

> *I always hope that it will find life worth living, and that it will live long to better and to beautify the earth. I hope it will love the blue sky and the white clouds passing by. I trust it will welcome all seasons and ever join merrily in the music, the motion, and the movement of the elemental dance with the winds. I hope it will live with rapture in the flower-opening days of spring and also enjoy the quiet summer*

rain. I hope it will be a home for the birds and hear their low, sweet mating-songs. I trust that when comes the golden peace of autumn days, it will be ready with fruited boughs for the life to come. I never fail to hope that if this tree is cut down, it may be used for a flagpole to keep our glorious banner in the blue above, or that it may be built into a cottage where love will abide; or if it must be burnt, that it will blaze on the hearthstone in a home where children play in the firelight on the floor.

He told audiences about the clear-cutting of Colorado's forests that he witnessed firsthand, estimating that barely 6,000 square miles of untouched woodland remained in the state out of "36,000 square miles of the finest timber land in the West," an article in the *Greeley Tribune* reported about one of his lectures. "Fire and the almost equally devastating sawmill have done their work well."

He connected the dots for those who attended his talks, explaining the consequences of inaction that could affect their own livelihoods and wallets: "the inevitable rise of the price of lumber, the driving away of tourist business from Colorado, and the even more important matter of destroying the natural water preserves. . . . Let the mountains once be denuded completely of forest growth, and the plentiful supply of water for irrigation that now comes down streams, will be reduced by at least one-half."

Mills's knowledge of forestry and its effects in Colorado and beyond led him to accept an appointment as the only federal lecturer on forestry, by Gifford Pinchot, the first head of the US Forest Service, in 1907. For the better part of two and a half years, the United States government picked up the tab for his lectures across the country, an endeavor he had already pursued for several years on his own dime—so the new position provided an even larger platform for his message about saving open lands in their pristine, natural form. Now he made bolder steps toward his goals and began to effect change on a national scale.

"Kansas City impresses me as being a very busy city—a progressive city—but you need more trees," he told the *Kansas City Star* in March 1907. "Every state should have a forestry commission. In Pennsylvania an

Keeping the Rocky Mountains pristine became Enos Mills's lifework.
CAROL HIGHSMITH, NATIONAL PARK SERVICE

appropriation of $500,000 annually is made to purchase mountain lands and encourage forestry. A forestry commission is needed in Kansas."

His lectures took him across the country, but even as he carried his message from coast to coast, he kept close watch on the proceedings at home in Estes Park and the wilderness preservation ideas gaining traction there. F. O. Stanley and town organizer C. H. Bond formed the Estes Park Protective and Improvement Association, with the goals of building more roads, trails to provide footpaths into the wilderness, a fish hatchery, and rules and laws to protect wildflowers from overgrazing by domestic livestock. They succeeded in establishing the fish hatchery, introducing literally millions of trout into the area's waterways, and they built what we now know as Fall River Road as well as trails up Prospect and Deer Mountains.

Creation of boundaries for a game preserve also rose to the top of this organization's list of tasks. Here Mills found himself in direct conflict with H. N. Wheeler, head of the Colorado Forest Service, who supervised the

Colorado (now Roosevelt) National Forest until 1921. Wheeler agreed that attracting tourists would be beneficial to the region, and he believed that a fairly small game reserve would do the trick. As a Forest Service representative, he felt that the regulations in place for timber harvesting and cattle ranching were adequate to protect the land, while he welcomed water diversion efforts to bring resources to farmlands, the opening of new mines, and trail construction throughout Estes Park. Wheeler also asserted that since there was no oversight body looking after the national parks already created, these natural areas suffered from neglect and unregulated use.

These uses did not meet Enos Mills's idea of sweeping preservation, however, and he spoke out against Wheeler's approach to preservation. Sometime within this public controversy, Mills began referring to the ultimate solution as a national park.

He wrote a statement that became his rallying cry, first listing the unique features of the area around Estes Park and describing "mountain scenes of exceptional beauty and grandeur," and then asserted:

> *In many respects this section is losing its wild charms. Extensive areas of primeval forests have been misused and ruined; saw-mills are humming and cattle are in the wild gardens! The once numerous big game have been hunted out of existence and the picturesque beaver are almost gone.*
>
> *These scenes are already extensively used as places of recreation. If they are to be permanently and more extensively used and preserved, it will be necessary to hold them as public property and protect them within a national park.*

With the solution crystallized in his own mind, Mills now turned to the news media to make his case for a national park. He defined the boundaries of this park to be "twenty-four miles to the north and south . . . from east to west thirty-two miles," in an article in the January 16, 1910, issue of the *Longmont Ledger*. (Over time, the latter dimension grew to forty-two miles.) On February 4, 1910, he clarified his idea further, promising that private landholders within the park boundaries would keep their land and holdings. The rest of the land already belonged to the government, he explained, so "no one will have a chance to sell land to the government, nor will the government meddle with mining, lumbering or any other enterprise." Instead, turning Estes Park into a national property "would promptly give it an excellent system of roads and trails," which would facilitate "[b]etter protection of the forest against fire." Hunting would be prohibited, allowing animals to thrive and sustain their populations.

"Not everyone realizes that climate and scenery together form one of Colorado's important assets," he concluded. "If this asset is to be productive our hills must have roads and trails; and for permanent productivity the scenery must be preserved. Make Estes a National Park and you will preserve and improve its scenery, make the region more productive at once and hasten the development of this section. This would help everyone in the state. Who would it injure?"

If the newspapers are to be believed, the new park's benefits would far outweigh its drawbacks. One writer expressed a fervent hope that a rule would be established "by which any one could pick what flowers they please but must leave the root. We have spoken of this matter before in these columns. It is pure thoughtlessness when the root is jerked out of the ground, for that cannot be replaced without considerable trouble in replanting the weed." When Mills spoke at a luncheon of the Denver Chamber of Commerce in November 1910, his declaration that "the time of the gun had passed and the automobile and camera had taken its place," met with "hearty applause," according to the reporter who covered it for the *Longmont Ledger*.

By the end of 1910, Mills told the *Lincoln Daily Star*, "We are near success," as he visited Denver for a Chamber of Commerce meeting. "The citizens and press of Greeley, Fort Collins, Loveland and Longmont have given unanimous indorsement [*sic*]. The newspapers of the largest cities and several magazines of the east have devoted columns of space to Estes park and have declared in favor of making it a national preserve. ... If Estes park be converted into grazing land the flowers will disappear in a few years, probably never to return. The national park would attract thousands of tourists here. It would aid in the good roads movement.

It would advertise the state as never before." He told the media he was sure that Congress would take up the question of a new national park in Colorado in its upcoming session.

This did not happen, however, and in September 1911, Secretary of Agriculture James Wilson paid a visit to Denver, bringing with him a news bombshell: He told officials that he had received a number of letters in opposition to the proposed national park. "The chief opposition to the plan seems to have come from those who have mining claims within the borders," the *Greeley Tribune* reported. There were others who protested the plan as well: Neighbors to Mills's own homestead in the shadow of Longs Peak questioned his motives, coming forward under the name of the Front Range Settlers' League. Mills resolved to make the demand for the park come from outside the state as well as within, and he took to the road, traveling cross-country for months to generate interest among the general public, the media, and influential politicians who might help his cause.

Another year passed before a report by the US Geological Survey, authored by Robert B. Marshall, gave a glowing recommendation to the US government to set aside seven hundred square miles of the region around Longs Peak as Rocky Mountain National Park. This left out three hundred square miles of the land Mills had sought to protect, keeping it open for active mining operations in progress there, but Mills apparently chose to accept a partial win rather than object to the compromise.

The bill to establish the park was introduced in Congress on February 6, 1913, by Congressman Edward Taylor, thus prying the lid off the barrel of objections that had lain dormant during the advocacy phase of the project. All kinds of claims to the land surfaced, killing the bill twice in committee over the next two years as local and state officials and congressmen worked to sort through and satisfy as many of the objectors as they could. The final bill did not come to the committee floor until the end of 1914, and by then the park's acreage had been cut in half, leaving just 358.5 square miles of parkland . . . but when the bill finally passed on January 18, 1915, its advocates were only too happy to declare a victory.

The *Denver Post* dubbed Mills "The Father of Rocky Mountain National Park," a moniker that became his legacy. And while he would have been the first to give credit to dozens of others who worked closely with him along the way, Mills's name is the one that remains on his crowning achievement. In his lifetime, he wrote fifteen books, climbed the highest mountains in Colorado, founded and led outdoor advocacy organizations, spoke before tens of thousands of people, and learned enough about the natural world to be considered the foremost authority about everything in the park; but we remember Enos Mills most reverently when we drive through any entrance of Rocky Mountain National Park and see the dense woodlands, soaring mountain peaks, expansive meadows, and wandering wildlife that attract more than 4.4 million people to this park every year.

The Birth of the Dude Ranch

In 1986, James D. Mote completed a Historic Structure Report and Historic Furnishing Study of Holzwarth Homestead in Rocky Mountain National Park, one of the only structures remaining after the park completed a massive deconstruction of buildings and mines within the park's boundaries. Maintained as a historic site, the Holzwarth property once included what many historians believe was Colorado's first dude ranch. Holzwarth did not keep a journal or other written records and the family did a superlative job of avoiding the press, so Mote compiled an oral history by interviewing Johnnie Holzwarth Jr., son of the original homesteader, about his parents' lives in Grand Lake and their homestead, ranch, and guest accommodations. I have used his account to reconstruct what life may have been like for this hardy German couple and their first-generation-American son there in the shadow of the Never Summer Mountains.

ON JANUARY 1, 1916, A CHANGE SWEPT THROUGH COLORADO THAT would close businesses and force citizens into one of two ways of life: either clean living and sobriety in every aspect of their existence or a clean exterior hiding a dark, law-breaking secret behind closed doors. That change was Prohibition, an era in which manufacturing and selling liquor suddenly became a crime. Taverns shut their doors, makers of beer and distilled spirits drained their equipment and shelved it, and drinking went underground, as people who had every intention of continuing to enjoy their libations found places to do this that law enforcement officers would never detect.

John Holzwarth found himself without a livelihood. He tried for a year to run his tavern—the Old Corner, on Santa Fe Drive in downtown

Denver—as a grocery store, but that proved unsuccessful and by early 1917, the building stood empty, its sign gone and its windows staring blankly into space.

He'd engaged in other professions since he arrived in the United States in 1879 at the age of fourteen with his brother, David, from their native Rudelsberg, Germany, but his days as an apprentice baker were now thirty-six years behind him, and he no longer had the stamina to work as a ranch hand, as he had done after his apprenticeship. He'd picked up skills as a trail cook and saloonkeeper during his two years of ranching in Texas, New Mexico, and southern Colorado, and also while working as a cook for the Texas Rangers and in a saloon in Las Vegas, New Mexico. These skills would serve him well for decades, on and off, but what he yearned to take up again was ranch life.

Decades earlier, in 1883, he had made the attempt to settle down near Stillwater, south of Grand Lake, an area now covered by Lake Granby. His brother David had already settled here and made a living driving the mail stage, so John had good reason to choose this community for his home. He lived on his eighty-acre ranch for ten years, working to establish a cattle and horse business, and making the most of his skills as a true western cowboy.

Businesses fail for all kinds of reasons, so it's hard to say why John Holzwarth's ranch did not thrive despite his knowledge and ability. Chances are that the failing silver mining industry cast enough of a pall over the Grand Lake area that a peripheral business such as raising beef would struggle as well. Whatever went wrong, Holzwarth knew when it was time to cut his losses. When he still had not managed to turn a profit by 1893, he packed up and moved to Denver to seek a more lucrative endeavor.

He managed to snag a job right away at the Tivoli Brewing Company, and he soon rose to the position of bottling foreman. Freed of the constant pressure of managing a ranch, he found himself with free time in the evenings, so he attended the Turnverein, a German social club, at the suggestion of other Germans living in Denver and working at the brewery. One evening, Holzwarth's coworker, Frank Lebfromm, decided to introduce John to his sister, Sophie. She had arrived in Denver three years earlier from Nussbach, Germany, when she was twenty years old, and she worked as a housekeeper—what her son later described as something more like indentured servitude—for some of the wealthiest families in the area.

As they were both from southern Germany, John and Sophie had an immediate connection, and a year later they were married. They had five children, though only three survived into adulthood: Julia, the oldest, born in 1896; Sophia, born in 1900; and John Jr., born in 1902, whom everyone called Johnnie to distinguish him from his father.

Despite their first child's birth, 1896 turned out to be a tough year for the couple, just two years into their marriage. John contracted typhoid fever, which debilitated him for some time, forcing him to give up work and spend down whatever savings the couple had scraped together. He had no choice but to sell off his Stillwater property and all of its equipment for a paltry six hundred dollars, which allowed them to pay bills while he recuperated. Once back on his feet, John and Sophie decided to pursue a mutual dream, and they leased a saloon from Neff Brewery and opened the Old Corner. Soon they were making a good living, and by the end of the first decade of the 1900s, they had paid off their debts and bought two double houses in the saloon's adjacent neighborhood.

Now they had the multiple streams of income that can elevate people from workaday lives into the upper middle class. In 1906, Sophie packed up Sophia and Johnnie and took them to Germany to visit their grandparents, and John went later to return to his hometown and see his parents. The future looked rosy for the young family, even as the state legislature argued over temperance and toyed with the idea of Prohibition.

Then the legislature took action, Prohibition became law, and turning the bar into a grocery store turned out to be nowhere near as profitable as selling alcohol. John and Sophie decided it was time to try something completely different.

Julia, for her part, determined her path in life fairly early on. She attended the Barnes School of Business in Denver, learned accounting and other marketable skills, gained some real-world work experience at Gates Rubber Company and Schwayder Truck Company—which later turned to luggage and owned the Samsonite brand—and landed her best position yet at the Hilb Company. Here she made her professional home, and over time she became the credit manager and treasurer of this ready-to-wear wholesaler long before women were usually seen outside of the office steno pool. Her talent with managing money extended to her own affairs as well. "Julia saved and invested wisely and turned out to be the financial anchor of the family," James Mote wrote in his report.

John headed north by northwest to Grand Lake and claimed a piece of land about ten miles north of the town on the eastern side of the Never Summer Mountains. He'd chosen rugged country, the mountains rising high enough to block the sun by late afternoon, but the Colorado River ran along his land to the east, promising a permanent water supply even in arid weather, and roads built to reach the 1890s mining towns already ran in his direction. In addition to his land, he bought another 160 acres next door—the homestead of Joseph Fleshuts, who abandoned the property in 1911 and vanished from history—for two thousand dollars, money he had available when he sold the saloon building, all of its fixtures, and one of the two duplexes—and he continued to collect rent for the second duplex. This gave him enough to cover the family's living expenses for some time until the new ranch began to turn a profit. With Sophie at his side and the wisdom of many years of running a business now at his disposal, Holzwarth had no doubt he would make a go of it this time.

BACK AT THE RANCH

John had a different concept for his ranch in 1917 from his original cattle and horse operation in 1883. Now he saw the opportunity that hospitality offered, and he planned to build cabins beyond his family's homestead and invite tourists looking for a sporting holiday to the property.

While Sophie stayed in Denver managing their remaining duplex and tending to her chickens and vegetable garden, and Johnnie, who was fourteen and had left school after eighth grade, worked odd jobs in the city, John began work on the first cabin. "The original structure consisted only of what is now the front room," wrote Mote. "It had a sod roof and in those first years was little more than a shelter against the elements.

The north half was partitioned into a bedroom for Mama and Papa, and Johnnie had a sleeping corner in the south half."

Construction of other structures continued in 1918, but in 1919, John met with a life-changing event. He was driving a horse wagon when it got caught going past a tree, and it threw him clear onto the rocky ground. He broke both legs and one hip, a debilitating accident for a young man and devastating for a man in his middle fifties. From then on, John needed canes to walk, and he struggled when trying to help build additional structures or tend to their hayfields. "His dream of developing a working ranch had to be totally abandoned," Mote said.

But Holzwarth kept moving. He assisted his family in any way he could with the maintenance and upkeep of the fishing cabins Johnnie continued to build on the property, with Sophie managing the reservations and guest services. "Through the 1920s, he took up taxidermy and woodworking," Mote said. "The deer-hoof coat hooks and stools still present in the 'Mama' cabin attest to his success at his new-found hobbies."

After John G. Holzwarth suffered a serious injury, he focused on taxidermy in this shop. LIBRARY OF CONGRESS

From 1919 until 1929, Johnnie, Julia, and Sophia took on most of the running of the homestead and other properties, under their mother's careful supervision. They remodeled the tent house they'd built in 1918 into a bunkhouse, and soon filled it nightly.

"One Sunday afternoon I caught 150 fish for friends of my father," Johnnie said in a rare press interview with Richard Johnson of *Empire Magazine* in 1974. "They had come up from Denver to visit. They gave my dad a quart of whiskey, and he got sick and puked all over everything, and my mother had to clean up the mess. On top of that, these guys got in a fight over how they were going to divide the fish. But when they left, they gave me a $5 bill. My mother and I got together, and she said, 'From now on, we're going to charge.'"

That was in 1919, and soon Sophie and her children had created the Holzwarth Trout Lodge, a center of hospitality for the fishermen and others who passed through, as well as for the community of Grand Lake. They rented out rooms to fishermen for the first time in 1920, taking overflow from Squeaky Bob Wheeler's Hardscrabble Lodge down the road. Charging two dollars a day or eleven dollars for a weeklong stay, the Holzwarths housed their guests in cabins they added to the property, and Mama Holzwarth, as she became known to her guests, furnished three meals a day at $1.50 per meal in the German-style dining room. "No one who ever knew Sophia Holzwarth can forget her vivacity, her gay humor, or her genuine hospitality," wrote Cairns in *Grand Lake in the Olden Days*. "No afternoon caller ever left her home without food and coffee; if there were not enough varieties of cookies, or if the coffee-cake seemed a wee bit stale, a fresh batch must be baked before the visitor departed." Dinner usually included trout caught in the river nearby, local venison and grouse Johnnie hunted, eggs and milk from the family's livestock, potatoes and greens grown on the premises, and home-baked biscuits.

Johnnie found that both the homestead and the hospitality life appealed to him much more than he had imagined they would. "As a city kid, I didn't think I'd stay there very long," he told Johnson. "But we learned to take punishment. We had to take it."

He bought a sawmill in 1923 for six hundred dollars and taught himself to use it, building a barn, sheds for storage, and more cabins. "The

Hilltop Manor became one of the main hospitality buildings at Holzwarth Trout Lodge. LIBRARY OF CONGRESS

neighbors were our teachers," he said. "One taught me horses. One taught me carpentry. And Squeaky Bob taught me how to keep house."

The obliging proprietor of one of Grand Lake's most popular lodges showed Johnnie how to wash dishes and split wood, things the young man thought he could do just fine. "The first time I washed dishes for him and scalded them, Squeaky Bob yelled, 'Hey, you don't scald dishes that way. You eat out of the inside, not out of the back. So scald the inside.'"

He took Bob's advice about wood chopping to heart as well. "He taught me to throw the wood so it was all straight up and down, in a kind of pyramid, so that when it rained, the water ran off and the wood drained properly."

Life lessons like these prepared Johnnie for what was coming up: the day when he would turn his parents' group of guest cabins into Never Summer Ranch, the first establishment of its kind in Colorado.

"I TAKE CARE OF MY DUDES"

With a loan of $13,500 from his sister Julia in 1928, Johnnie began the process of expanding the Trout Lodge into a ranch for people who wanted to enjoy Rocky Mountain National Park on horseback. He married in 1931 and moved next door, continuing to develop the ranch with the seasonal help of his sister Sophia and her family, who lived in Denver but spent summers at the ranch. Sophia's husband, Andrew Geeck, brought his skills with repair work to the family enterprise, and her two daughters worked there as well.

They offered their guests what they called the American Plan, charging $5.00 to $5.50 per person per day for a room near a bathroom ($4.50 for double occupancy), and $6.00 to $7.00 daily for a room with a private bath. Weekly fees started at $28.00 and rose to a still-affordable $45.00 if guests did not want to share a bathroom with strangers. Families could choose a cabin instead, "attractively furnished, private bath, fireplace and porch," according to the lodge's first advertising literature, with half rates for children. All room and cabin fees included Mama Holzwarth's substantial meals three times daily.

In addition to the pleasures of spending days or weeks in one of the nation's most magnificent wilderness areas, Holzwarth's offered a number of pastimes and activities: a twenty-eight-mile trip by automobile at dawn, "fries" on Sunday evenings (presumably Rocky Mountain oysters, which are cattle testicles), rodeos in season, swimming in Grand Lake, dancing, croquet, horseshoes, ping-pong, archery, shuffleboard, and guided horseback pack trips. Daily mail, telephone, and telegraph service ensured that visitors did not have to lose touch with home during their western vacation. "Sport clothes are always in order," the brochure informed potential guests. "Blue jeans, riding boots, colorful shirts, sweaters and a warm top coat for cool evenings. Guests come to meals in riding or sport clothes. A dressy wardrobe is unnecessary. Bring your camera!"

To get to the lodge, visitors could take the Denver and Salt Lake Railway to Granby and ride to the resort from the station in the Holzwarth car for a nominal fee, or take the bus from Denver. "Easterners can leave New York by plane and arrive at Holzwarth's the following day for lunch," the literature said.

The short hospitality season began in mid-June and ended by mid-September or the first of October, the only part of the year when chances were good that visitors would not have to wade through snow to get there. In winter, only John and Johnnie remained at the homestead, while the rest of the family returned to Denver. "There was no electricity," Mote said. "Light came from kerosene and coal-oil lamps. . . . There was no running water and no indoor plumbing. Johnnie did dig a well under the kitchen floor when the addition was added to the Mama cabin in 1921, which brought water via a hand pump into the kitchen." They had featherbedding on both of their beds, and a battery-powered RCA radio, but "otherwise, [Johnnie] and his father read many Zane Grey novels by kerosene lamp on winter evenings." It took just $125.00 for the two men to live through the winter, enough to pay their property taxes and buy enough food to keep the pantry stocked until spring. If they needed more, Johnnie did odd jobs—the worst of which, he later recalled, involved cutting ice on the surface of Grand Lake and loading it onto wagons to sell to other homesteaders for their iceboxes. He also trapped beaver and ermine for their furs, which fetched good prices in the hundreds of dollars every winter.

When John Holzwarth died in 1932, Mama and Johnnie changed the operation of their guest accommodations, terminating the American Plan and installing cook stoves in the cabins so guests could cook for themselves and do their own housekeeping. This freed Mama to cook at the larger dude ranch, while the younger Sophia assisted with the upkeep of the cabins.

Throughout the 1930s, Johnnie continued to improve the facilities at the ranch. He built a dining hall, a lodge, and a barn, and created guided excursions for visitors to take them to the most spectacular views on horseback. He added running water in the 1940s with a gravity-fed water service as well as indoor bathrooms in the cabins and electricity on the homestead. When Mama Holzwarth passed away in 1952, Johnnie intended to modernize the property even further, but his sister Sophia objected, apparently with the belief that the ranch's attraction had much to do with its authentically rustic western style. This dedication to preserving the site as it was played a role in its eventual purchase by the

Holzwarth's cabins gave trout fishermen and tourists a comfortable, if rustic, place to stay. LIBRARY OF CONGRESS

National Park Service in 1971, with the park's commitment to keeping a part of the property as a "living homestead."

Johnnie did make one major change, however: He sold his cattle, moving away from maintaining the property as a working ranch. "I went to a cattleman and said, 'I don't like my cattle,'" he told Johnson at *Empire*. "And he said, 'What position does your cattle stand?' And I said, 'Oh, I take care of my dudes first, and then my sawmill, and then my cattle.' He said, 'You've got third-rate cattle.' So I sold them."

Johnnie agreed to sell the ranch and homestead to the park for $1.625 million, granting him a comfortable retirement. By this time his first wife—Caroline, with whom he raised a son and a daughter— had died, but he remarried later on and kept three homes in Colorado, including the twenty acres he still enjoyed at the Never Summer Ranch by agreement with the Park Service.

Visitors enjoyed this expansive view from the Holzwarth property. CAROL HIGHSMITH, NATIONAL PARK SERVICE

Today the Holzwarth Historic Site tells the story of one hardworking family's experience in the Colorado Rockies, a slice of life that has become part of the fabric of the American West. Volunteers well-versed in the lifestyle of this original dude ranch can answer virtually any question about the lives of those whose innovations in hospitality fostered an entire industry in Colorado, a new way to vacation with all of the rigors of ranching and the pleasures of home.

The Highest Road

To appreciate the scope of this endeavor, one must remember the main ingredient in the accomplishment of the work was brawn, tempered by a tough and willing work ethic. It was done without benefit of the bulldozer, which was just coming onto the scene. This may be a surprise to the people today who believed bulldozers came with the territory. The work force were tough, skilled, and resourceful. They were expert powdermen, stone masons, timbermen, and machine operators. They knew how [to] drill and control blasting to most efficiently reduce the rock excavation to rubble without littering and damaging the adjacent landscape. All of this and there was not one hard hat on the entire operation! Also there were no fatalities.

—Daniel C. Harrington
Inspector, Bureau of Public Roads

Once Rocky Mountain National Park secured the official protection of the National Park Service in 1915, residents in the area may have believed that federal funding would rain down on the park for the construction of amenities like bridges, trails, and roads. The reality was quite different, however: The first entity to build roads within the park was not the US government but the state of Colorado.

Construction of Fall River Road began in 1913, while legislation to create the park roamed through Congress on its long journey to passage. The finished road, financed by Larimer and Grand Counties as well as the state, would provide the first path from Estes Park to Grand Lake on which wagons and automobiles could traverse the area easily, with the goal of accommodating tourists as well as residents. When news reached local legislators at the end of 1915 that Rocky Mountain had become a national park, only a short stretch of the road had reached completion, penetrating the park just a few miles from the Estes Park side. The work took on new urgency with the knowledge that more tourists would be coming their way, but it still took five years—until 1920—before Fall River Road united the park's two entrance towns.

In 1919, National Park Service director Stephen Mather noted in his annual report to the Department of the Interior that the state of Colorado had invested two hundred thousand dollars in "improving the entrance roads to Rocky Mountain Park, which they will undoubtedly pave a little later, this in addition to the construction of the Fall River Road, which is being built over the Continental Divide connecting the east and west sides of the park."

Fall River Road takes visitors through dense woodlands, past streams and tumbling waterfalls, and into the heart of wildlife country, where visitors can see elk, coyotes, and even black bears at a proximity rarely available in wide grassy areas like Sheep Lakes. If you've ever driven the part of this road that remains in the park to this day, you know the two most important things about it: First, the special experience of seeing the park's high country from this secluded road has no equal; and second, it's darned scary to drive it. The single-lane road, while well-maintained and as smooth as a dirt road can get, nonetheless remains a dirt road loaded with tight switchbacks, including a couple of hairpin turns that require larger vehicles to perform K-turns to navigate. For some visitors, this can serve as a quintessential national park experience; for those who feel squeamish about roads with no shoulders, steep grades, and foliage that can reach right into a car's open windows, Fall River Road may put too much "wild" in their wilderness.

Back before there were Subaru Foresters, of course, visitors driving through Rocky Mountain rode in touring cars with wire or metal wheels that more closely resembled bicycle wheels than today's rugged radials (take a look at www.earlyamericanautomobiles.com to see what cars of the decade were like). Many of these vehicles did not have roofs, and none of them had safety features like seat belts. "Some motorists were too

Switchbacks like these make driving Fall River Road a tricky endeavor.
LIBRARY OF CONGRESS

frightened to drive over the road, and others found their vehicles could not negotiate the grade on account of low gear rations or gravity-feed fuel systems," noted the Historical American Engineering Record (HAER) in 1993.

Mather knew that construction of paved roads within the parks would make them more accessible to visitors, which in turn would draw visitors who could drive to the nation's most magnificent scenery. He emphasized the importance of this, but in the same breath, he noted, "Although there has been such tremendous activity in the construction of roads in the national park States, practically no money has been available for road extensions in the national parks this year," with the exception of some repairs in Yosemite. "In some parks the funds available have not even been sufficient to prevent perceptible deterioration." He went on to insist that the roads within the parks needed to be paved roads—not simply dirt roads—affirming that "motorists visiting our parks have a right to demand from the Government, as they do, as good, if not better, roads in the national parks than are furnished by the States and counties as approaches to the parks, especially as the Government exacts an entrance fee from the automobile owners for using the park roads."

With exactly this goal in mind, Rocky Mountain superintendent Roger W. Toll determined that a new road was in order. He imagined that this road would begin at the Moraine Park Road on the east side of the park and would follow the Trail Ridge—the route the Paleoindians and the Ute had used to cross the Continental Divide for millennia—to the Fall River Pass. He shared this vision with the National Park Service, but several years would pass before Rocky Mountain received part of a $7.5 million allocation to the Park Service for road construction; only then did it become possible to plan a longer, higher route that made the park more accessible to drivers and their families.

By this time, the National Park Service understood the need to set standards for architecture and design throughout all of the parks under its supervision. It had hired a staff of architects and landscape designers, some of whom took over the supervision of road design. Thomas Vint became chief landscape architect for the entire national park system. A man who had studied at the University of California, Berkeley, and

Logs left by the side of the road were cleared by National Park Service and Civilian Conservation Corps crews. NATIONAL PARK SERVICE

understood the methods of naturalistic design developed by the arts and crafts movement, harmonizing building and road design with the natural surroundings, Vint saw the potential for applying this kind of architectural sensibility to buildings and roads within the parks, without compromising the functionality these projects required. "The materials, type of construction, and details . . . were determined by the natural qualities of each site," wrote Linda Flint McClelland in her book, *Preserving Nature: The Historic Landscape Design of the National Park Service 1916 to 1942*, "including climate, weather, presence of local stone or timber, topography, and the scale of surrounding forests."

At the same time, making park roads somewhat less intimidating to visitors became a priority. "Park road designers endeavored to eliminate the hazardous curves, sharp turns, and steep inclines that characterized mountain roads," said McClelland. "Switchbacks on most roads were gradually replaced by radial curves."

W. L. Lafferty, of the national Bureau of Public Roads (BPR), became the resident engineer on the project, and the first section of the road, connecting the Fall River Road in Horseshoe Park with Deer Ridge, got underway in June 1926. It included a reinforced concrete bridge faced in native stone, making it a complementary part of the landscape while providing the strength and durability required for heavy use. With this in place by October, the project moved on to the major portion of the road from Deer Ridge to Grand Lake, beginning with a survey team who would decide on the route the road would take through the terrain, with an eye toward achieving "more moderate grades, gentler curves, fewer places of heavy snow accumulation, and better scenic opportunities" than Fall River Road, according to the HAER. The team included Toll; his assistant superintendent, Edmund Rogers; NPS landscape architect Howard Baker; and "Bull of the Woods" Steven A. Wallace, BPR location engineer, whose reputation for choosing locations for roads and railroads through difficult terrain had earned him his admiring nickname.

The survey began in the fall of 1926 and continued into the spring, with the four men riding in on horses, setting up camps six miles apart, and carrying surveying equipment and other supplies back and forth from each camp to shorten the time and distance they had to cover each

Engineers tempered the severity of sharp curves by directing them along mountain ridges, like this one at Rainbow Curve. LIBRARY OF CONGRESS

day. Wallace made additional trips into the park in winter to observe snow accumulation and determine the potential for avalanches along the route he'd chosen. His final plan allowed visitors to continue to use Fall River Road while the new road was under construction, and only a few sections would require heavy excavation. The road would have a grade of only 5 to 7 percent along its length, a major correction from Fall River Road's stretches of 16 percent grade. Switchback curves would be far gentler than Fall River Road's jackknife curves as well. "Rather than follow the old road route over Forest Canyon Pass and down the steep switchbacks to Milner Pass, the new road was to drop around a single switchback"—Medicine Bow Curve—"and follow a lower line down the ridge closer to the Cache la Poudre River, about half a mile northwest of the old road," the HAER said.

Overall, the new road would exceed the length of the old one, but the improvements in grade and easier curves would make up for the extra time. Wallace had made certain that the new Trail Ridge Road offered "unsurpassed mountain scenery, high mountains, deep canyons, many lakes and perpetual snow, alpine flower gardens and wooded areas all combining to make a trip over not to be forgotten."

Wallace's plan received extensive reviews from the highest levels of the BPR and the National Park Service, including NPS chief engineer Frank A. Kittredge, who had overseen construction of Going-to-the-Sun Road in Glacier National Park and road overhauls in Yosemite. He walked the route personally and made recommendations for changes, sending Wallace back into the field to resurvey some areas and incorporate Kittredge's insights. Finally, after nearly three years, the final plan received approval—and NPS director Horace Albright announced in 1929 that Rocky Mountain would receive $1.75 million to move forward with construction.

About two and a half miles of the planned route actually crossed into the Arapaho National Forest adjacent to the park's northwest corner, but in 1930, Rocky Mountain acquired 14,144 acres of this forest, securing the headwaters of the Colorado River in the Never Summer Mountains— "a magnificently scenic area," as Director Albright reported in his 1929–30 fiscal year annual report to the secretary of the interior.

Not everyone hailed the news of the road construction project with boundless enthusiasm. Robert Quillen, editorial essayist for Publisher's Syndicate, had this to say in November 1929: "For the commercialization of its scenic wonderlands, Colorado is to pay a price not reflected in highway construction contracts, federal appropriations and tax bills. The

Trail Ridge Road became one of the most scenic roads in the entire NPS system.
LIBRARY OF CONGRESS

price is the taming of the wilderness. One by one the state's beauty spots more or less inaccessible are to be opened up to cars in high gear. . . . Now the new Trail Ridge road between Grand Lake and Estes Park will pass Iceberg Lake. The chauffeur can drive his employer to its shores, and the Coloradoan must go further for scenes that thrill. The same new highway will go thru Hidden Valley. The thick undergrowth, the aspens, and the beautiful lake and huge beaver dam and house will survive this modern highway. The valley will remain, but it will be no longer hidden at the base of a narrow road. Thus it will lose much of its magic."

FOLLOWING THE CENTERLINE

Work on the 17.2-mile section from Deer Ridge to Fall River Pass began on September 28, 1929, with W. A. Colt and Son of Las Animas, Colorado, the contractor. "Colonel W. A. Colt was seventy-three years old when he received the award for the project," the HAER tells us. "Colt had built a number of other roads in high mountain passes, including the road over Wolf Creek Pass (elev. 10,850) in the San Juan Mountains of southwestern Colorado. He began his career working on the Erie Canal in the 1870s, then on the Texas & Pacific Railway and the Jay Gould Lines in Missouri. He also constructed the St. Louis, Iron Mountain & Southern Railroad." With experience at high elevations as well as closer to sea level, Colt knew what kinds of challenges his crews would face working in the thin air of mountain passes; his railroad work taught him how to handle a project that involved following the engineers' staked-out centerline faithfully for many miles and moving his camps and equipment on a regular basis.

The Colt crews, a contingent of forty-five men, built a mobile camp of "composition board nailed to wooden frames," with tar paper roofs, making it easy to disassemble and relocate down the road. They positioned the temporary buildings in the right-of-way so as not to cause any lasting damage to the roadside vegetation and rock formations. "Even a moveable road camp could not stay close to the early clearing and grubbing crews," the HAER noted, "and one worker later recalled that Colt worked three crews—one working, one leaving, and one on the way!" A separate camp hosted the masons and concrete workers once the first crew cleared the land and excavated the path of the new road.

Trees had to be felled, and the crews stacked timber alongside the roadway that could be removed by the park and milled for building construction. A mild winter allowed them to keep working through December and January, finishing the tree and brush clearing along the entire route before February while a single steam shovel worked its way up the route, completing five miles of "pioneering" ground excavation. A gas-powered shovel arrived in February to excavate the harder rock, while eight dump trucks removed load after load of rubble.

Winter weather finally set in in March, suspending work for three weeks and prompting Colt to put an additional gas shovel on the job when they resumed operations in April. The onset of winter had frozen the ground at the higher elevations, so excavation had to be confined to the lower sections of the road, but enough had been cleared to allow a small crew to start building box culverts of reinforced concrete in two places at the east end of the road.

"As road crews began work above timberline, a number of problems were encountered," noted the HAER. "Normal drills would not penetrate the frozen tundra, and new equipment had to be designed. Harsh weather and the thin air over 11,000' made heavy labor difficult. High winds and snowstorms hampered operations."

Masonry contractors built culverts like this one by hand, using local stone.
LIBRARY OF CONGRESS

On June 1, Colt brought in a fourth gas shovel to begin excavation at Fall River Pass, working eastward. "By mid-August, it had prepared a rough grade extending east from the pass for four miles and began rock excavation on the intervening section," the HAER said. Soon a fifth gas shovel came in to speed progress from the west end, while a dozen men worked with two tractors, a grader and four horses, removing large rocks from the right-of-way, trimming slopes and digging ditches. Another twelve men worked on "hand-laid rock embankments."

"The work is approximately 40 percent completed," Director Albright reported to the US secretary of the interior in his annual report that summer, after making a trip to the park in June to inspect the progress to date. "The west-side Fall River project of 10 miles, running from Fall River Pass to the Colorado River, has been advertised, and it is expected that the contract will be let and construction begun before the close of the present season." Vint, Kittredge, and a series of BPR engineers also visited, and Kittredge and a National Park Service assistant engineer named A. van V. Dunn even took a day to climb Longs Peak during their stay.

August brought the first heavy work on what became known as Rock Cut, a segment of road where a projecting rock mountainside had to be removed, creating a massive granite wall on one side of the pavement. At 12,110 feet in elevation, the roadway through this area presented its own set of challenges, so blasting through so much rock made it the most complex demolition and construction project on the Trail Ridge route.

Work began with a drill rig and compressor, with a gas shovel working farther west at Iceberg Pass. Here the alpine tundra received special attention as eleven men worked to protect this fragile ecosystem while grading a road through the middle of it. Ten more men dug ditches and did finishing work, while a third crew of ten placed pipe culverts, and a fourth crew of twenty-four men built the rock embankments by hand. By the end of August, the work force included "a project superintendent, six foremen, eight shovel operators, eight oilers, five cooks, three blacksmiths, two mechanics, and one hundred and fifty laborers," the HAER said. "The major equipment included five gas shovels, the Ingersoll-Rand compressor and four portable air compressors, three tractors, three blades, four fresnos [horse-drawn scrapers], twenty trucks and eight horses."

Blasting through the mountain wall to create Rock Cut proved to be the most challenging part of building Trail Ridge Road. LIBRARY OF CONGRESS

Drilling would not be enough to remove all of the rock the project required, however. The tried-and-true solution was black powder, a powerful explosive substance that could break solid granite into thousands of shards small enough to be cleared away with a steam shovel. Blasting crews generally used thirty shots at once to remove rock, but in this case, they had to use many more shots than usual to make the required impact. At one point, they wired together a total of 178 shots—about 1,000 pounds of black powder—to remove a section of the mountain, an amount the HAER considered "immense."

So much blasting sent rocks hurtling in every direction, creating the potential for damage to other parts of the mountainside and the surrounding terrain. The crew counteracted this by building log walls around the nearest rock faces to prevent permanent scarring by boulders sailing through the air. Another crew retrieved large rocks that landed well beyond the blasting area, minimizing the disturbance to the overall landscape, and a steam shovel and dump trucks gathered the remaining debris and took it to be crushed for use as road surface.

On October 1, a major storm drove Colt's crews down from the top of the park, so they continued their work at lower elevations until winter's onset shut them down. Colt laid off most of his crew in mid-November until the following spring and attempted to continue working with a crew of just thirty men, but their equipment froze in the bitter cold, forcing them to cease operations by mid-December.

The spring of 1931 brought one winter storm after another and piled snow high along the entire Trail Ridge Road route, so much so that Colt could not bring his crews back in to continue working until the middle of June.

"Two crews of workmen, giant steam shovels and long lines of machinery are waiting in Estes Park ready to rush work to complete the new Trail Ridge road from Estes Park to Grand Lake as soon as frost, which makes the construction work impossible now, is thawed out of the ground," the *Greeley Tribune-Republican* reported in April. "Construction work which has proceeded thruout [*sic*] the year, following an old Indian trail through Hidden Valley along the top of the divide to the Fall River Pass and thence down the west side of the mountains to Grand Lake, has proceeded through storms, snow, freezing temperatures, and rocky cliffs almost impossible to blast into a roadway."

When work finally resumed, the crew tackled the toughest part of the job, a section of the route classified as 100 percent rock. Diligent work with a gas shovel and efficient cleanup crews clearing debris from embankments led to completion of the rough grading in August, a major milestone for the construction project.

Now Colt confirmed that he intended to finish the road that season, before the return of winter weather shut them down again in November. This renewed the pressure on the men struggling to complete the heaviest rock work in the project's middle section, and accusations flew between engineers on different crews. One blamed slow progress on shovels too light to handle the toughest rock and then decided that the men in charge of blasting didn't know what they were doing. A major winter storm on October 20 forced another work stoppage, but despite this and other obstacles, the project remained on schedule: 94 percent of the work was done, leaving less than a season's worth of tasks to be completed.

A. E. Palen, BPR district engineer, made an inspection visit that fall with BPR chief Thomas MacDonald and Thomas Vint. Palen spoke to the media in Denver after the trip and announced that the road would open in the summer of 1932. The media reacted with measured excitement.

"The maximum elevation reached is 12,185," the *Greeley Daily Tribune* reported, "and, though the road does not have the elevation of the Mount Evans Road, above Echo Lake, it is a thru thorofare [*sic*], which is not the case with the Mount Evans highway. For that reason, the Trail Ridge road will have the distinction of being the highest thru travel highway in the world."

In May 1932, crews removed the snow in the last section of the Trail Ridge route to allow the men to access the area and resume their work. They completed the finishing work on August 1, on schedule with eight days to spare. The construction of Trail Ridge Road from Deer Ridge to Fall River Pass had consumed $440,940.87, making it an on-time, on-budget project and a major success for the park.

THE WEST SIDE

While Colt and his crews labored along the eastern portion of the road, L. T. Lawler Company of Butte, Montana, won the bid for the work on the western end of the road from Fall River Pass to Kawuneeche Valley. Lawler had a history of satisfactory work projects in national parks and forests as well as some federal-aid highway projects. This crew took up residence at Phantom Valley Ranch, not far from Grand Lake, and began work on October 8, 1930, with ten men clearing the trees along the right-of-way and piling them along the roadside. Park staff then transported the logs to sawmills on horse-drawn skids for reuse as lumber in the park.

Lawler then moved in two gas shovels, four large portable air compressors with drills, three dump trucks, two service trucks, and smaller items, and he began the grading work on October 23. He got a good month in before heavy snows arrived at the end of November, shutting down construction until the following spring.

In April 1931, Lawler's men and park service employees cleared the snow from the route, and the contractor set to work once again, adding two power shovels, two more compressors, four jackhammers, two Caterpillar tractors, a Caterpillar nine-foot grader, and a welding machine to his complement of heavy machinery. Additional camps sprang up near Poudre Lakes and Fall River Pass, the latter of which became the portable camp that relocated along the route as required.

Once the weather truly broke, the work progressed quickly, as 160 men arrived to keep the project moving. The shovel crews completed nine of the ten miles of required grading, including digging out tree stumps, while tractors pulled out the ones hardest to reach. Another crew placed corrugated metal pipe culverts. On this side of the park, however, Lawler's men encountered different issues from the Colt crews: Wetlands around Poudre Lake made for difficult digging in swampland, requiring special equipment to remove ground for grading. The discovery of underground springs in one section created additional issues. In other areas, rocks and gravel piled by rockslides required more removal than they had scheduled. Permafrost in the higher elevations forced crews to strip the frozen soil away in layers as they exposed it to the air, taking off a few inches at a time from the top as the surface thawed. "Although this caused delays, the procedure worked better than blasting, as excavated material could be well utilized in embankments," the HAER explained. "If frozen material had been placed, an undue amount of settlement could have been expected."

It's a testament to the determination of these crews that one obstacle after another did not significantly slow their progress—by late October, when winter weather began to arrive in earnest, the clearing had been completed and only a small amount of excavation work remained for the following spring. "The contractor had completed 75 percent of the work but had consumed only 45 percent of his allotted time," the HAER said.

The masonry contractor, Oliver H. Lindstrom & Son, of Boulder, made excellent progress that season as well. Using aggregates from a pit in the Colorado River and stone from the south side of Little Sheep Mountain, they built 50 percent of the required culvert masonry, and used stone from a rockslide four miles below the road for the masonry headwalls.

On June 4, 1932, the crews were back at work, but they had new issues to contend with to keep up their efficient pace: Saturated ground in the swampy portion of the route required the crews to build platforms of timber or corduroy road, laying logs across the road to give the shovels a stable base from which to work. Here, too, mudslides became a major issue, refilling the cleared areas so that the crews had to dig them out again and again. To prevent this condition from destroying the finished road, the crew excavated much deeper than normal, digging out as much as four feet below grade and backfilling with gravel and rock from the mountains to allow rain and spring water to drain through. They directed heavy spring snowmelt runoff into rubble drains and ditches, preventing it from flooding the road every year.

With masonry work completed and the last four miles of the road in place, the project came to a rapid conclusion on August 23, a whopping 158 days ahead of schedule. The entire road had a crushed rock surface for the time being; paving with a "base surface" would come the following summer. Senior Highway Engineer Clyde E. Learned of the BPR praised the project after completing his inspection in September 1932:

The finished contract shows excellent workmanship throughout, the high cutbanks, especially in solid ledge rock, being true to line and presenting a very neat appearance. Uniformity has been built into the road throughout the entire section, both the inside and outside shoulders presenting neat and uniform lines. The masonry work in both the headwalls and box culverts shows excellent workmanship, and presents an artistic appearance. The Bureau's engineer and the contractor deserve considerable credit for this excellent piece of spectacular mountain road construction.

Trail Ridge Road became a model that even chief landscaper Herbert Maier of the National Park Service followed in defining park design across the country. As the first to be built according to the Park Service's new standards for excavation and masonry and with the highest standards to date for protection of the surrounding landscape, it served as an illustration of the success of these concepts, both for their use of natural materials and their ability to bring visitors closer to expansive mountain views, forests, streams, meadows, and wildlife without risking the destruction of these attractions. In fact, Maier included photos of Trail Ridge Road in a handbook distributed to district inspectors across the country to demonstrate what appropriate park road design looked like.

Director Albright praised the newly completed road in a visit to Estes Park on September 14, 1932. "In large measure the steady increase in travel which week after week broke all previous records in the park is due to the attractiveness of the new road," he said. "This national park here is facing a new era of development with the completion of the new road across the divide. Most majestic of all our parks, Rocky Mountain National is destined to gain the admiration of the largest numbers due to its proximity to the centers of population. Travel in the region will probably show a continuous increase in the region for many years to come."

"We Can Take It!" The Civilian Conservation Corps in Rocky Mountain

A great many of the young men have become proficient in work which offers a means of earning their future livelihood. Others have received a start in life that will undoubtedly be of great benefit to them in future years and which they may not have ever received had they not been fortunate enough to spend some months in the camps. The boys who have enrolled in the camps have learned habits that will be beneficial to them through the remainder of their lives. . . . At the end of the first six months in the camp the young man is alert, self-confident, hopeful, happy, with a confident swing in his body, ready and willing to face the world with renewed courage and energy, to take his place in our industrial or business life when the opportunity offers.

—Robert Fechner
Director, Civilian Conservation Corps

No initiative since the formation of the National Park Service in 1916 has had as profoundly positive an impact on America's parks as the Civilian Conservation Corps (CCC), the first of President Franklin Roosevelt's programs to put people to work in 1933. Launched just a month after Roosevelt's inauguration, the CCC—originally known as Emergency Conservation Work, or ECW—put hundreds of thousands of young men to work in parks, forests, and other open spaces, taking up the slack in job opportunities caused by the stock market crash in October 1929 and the resulting Great Depression.

With nearly 25 percent of the American labor force unemployed in 1933—that's a whopping 12.8 million people without jobs—Roosevelt acted quickly to put people to work in ways that would do more than put food on the table. The CCC relocated about three million young, unmarried men between the ages of eighteen and twenty-five from the nation's cities and towns and set them to work in more than 2,900 camps in America's wilderness areas. Many began their CCC activity by building their own accommodations, gaining practical skills they would be able to use in reducing the backlog of maintenance and construction projects in open lands across the country. With this preliminary task covered, they took on responsibilities as diverse as planting trees, building visitor centers and retaining walls, learning to fight fires, removing unused roads, destroying trees infected by parasitic beetles, constructing tables for campgrounds, and performing all manner of maintenance on existing structures.

The first men to arrive at Rocky Mountain battled the elements to set up camp in May 1933. NATIONAL PARK SERVICE

Rampant unemployment had plunged these men into poverty and want. "Enrollees came into the camps of the District, under-nourished and under-weight, disappointed, disheartened, of low morale, disgusted with the world in which they had found themselves, sick at heart because of economic conditions in their homes, and with the opinion that nothing was right with civilization," the 1936 report *A History of the Civilian Conservation Corps in Colorado* tells us.

Once arrived at a CCC camp, however, they found food in abundance, improving their strength and sense of well-being in a matter of days. They filled their lungs with fresh air free of the pollutants rampant in cities during the industrial age, and found themselves surrounded by natural sights so glorious that they could not help but be buoyed by the change in scenery. As CCC director Robert Fechner wrote in 1938, in an introduction to the book *History of the Civilian Conservation Corps, Colorado and Wyoming District*, the program had a humanitarian objective as well as an ecological one: "to give jobs to hundreds of thousands of discouraged and undernourished young men, idle through no fault of their own, to build up these young men physically and spiritually and to start the nation on a sound conservative program which would conserve and expand our timbered resources, increase recreational opportunities and reduce the annual toll taken by forest fire, disease, pests, soil erosion and floods."

The Conservation Emergency

Roosevelt had an unusually keen interest in seeing the nation's forests properly tended and nurtured. On his own property in Hyde Park, New York, along the banks of the Hudson River, he practiced the tenets of scientific forestry, managing a sustainable timber crop with a careful balance between environmental protection and harvesting. Long before he became president, he directed his staff to plant more than one million trees on the expansive lands around his family's mansion, creating a remarkably beautiful woodland that continues to be preserved according to the practices he put in place in the 1920s. Today Roosevelt's farm and forest are part of the Home of Franklin Delano Roosevelt National Historic Site, a National Park Service property, which is also the home of the FDR Presidential Library and Museum. (Should you ever make your way to New York, I encourage you to walk along the forest's well-maintained trails and see what Roosevelt accomplished, preserving a perfectly lovely patch of woodland in an area surrounded by encroaching development. I had the pleasure of exploring it for another of my books, a Falcon Guide titled *Hiking through History New York*.)

When Roosevelt became a New York state senator, he worked with the state forests commissioner to establish the New York Conservation Department, and he continued to put his interest in forestry to work as vice president of the New York State Forestry Association. Once in office in the White House, Roosevelt had an unprecedented opportunity to protect the entire country's forests in the way he wished to see them protected. He brought together four departments in his cabinet—Agriculture, Interior, Labor, and War—to administer the CCC program, requiring a level of cooperation that is hard to fathom in twenty-first-century politics. One representative of each department joined Fechner on an advisory council to determine how to proceed.

"It was the task of the advisory council to convert the half-billion acres of the nation's timbered domain into a vast workshop which would furnish employment and a new chance for a vast army of youngsters," Fechner wrote. This workforce would engage in projects "which would not only enhance the present value of our national resources but which would increase their usefulness to future generations."

Within three months of the establishment of the first camp—a 200-man installation in Luray, Virginia—the first enrollment of about 300,000 men, including 250,000 civilians, 25,000 war veterans, and 25,000 "experienced woodsmen," began to move across the map. Each received thirty dollars a month in wages, of which the government sent twenty-five dollars to their families back home. With food, clothing, and shelter provided to the workers, the remaining five dollars per month provided enough pocket money for modest entertainment and personal needs.

The men set to work under the supervision of the Department of the Interior and the US Army, which divided them into numbered companies living in camps. Several of these companies received Rocky Mountain National Park as their assignment, occupying four camps within the park and one just outside of it. Evidence of these camps became scarce very rapidly once the CCC members were called to the military in 1941, as the men themselves disassembled the buildings and removed the materials as trash, but park archaeologist William Butler explored the sites at Beaver Creek, Grand Lake, Little Horseshoe Park, and Mill Creek at length and prepared a report on his findings in 2006.

"The War Department, i.e. mainly the US Army, was responsible for the selection of men, construction of camps, and the delivery of supplies and equipment," Butler said. "Officers and enrollees quarters were initially army tents that were gradually replaced by more substantial wood structures. Inexpensive prefabricated building components were produced in 1934 when allowed for the efficient construction of several types of buildings." These relied on designs used in World War I on military installations.

The first unit to arrive here, Company 809, faced the daunting task of building a temporary camp in Little Horseshoe Park in early May—but initially, they found themselves thwarted by a late-season blizzard and had to bed down in the utility area until spring finally arrived. They finally built their barracks of large canvas tents—"pyramidal tents with wood supports were the norm," Butler noted—in the shadow of Big Horn Mountain, a gorgeously scenic spot they would occupy only through October. Three other companies would follow them in making this camp their spring and summer headquarters through 1939: Companies 802, 864, and 865.

Soon Company 1809 arrived to construct seasonal Camp NP-3. Records indicate that this camp stood about twelve miles north of Grand Lake on the Colorado River, perhaps on Beaver Creek, though its temporary buildings and the activity that took place there left little residue behind. The camp functioned for only two years in the spring, summer, and early fall of 1933 and 1934, and Company 1812 replaced Company 1809 in the second year. In 1935, Camp NP-7 was erected, and Companies 809, 847, and 808 used it in succession in the summers of 1935, 1938, and 1940.

Company 864, consisting of 127 men primarily from Arizona, arrived on May 15, 1934, and made their home base at Camp NP-4-C, a tent camp assembled "only a few miles from the beautiful village of

Estes Park, and almost at the foot of majestic Long's Peak," according to the narrative in *History of the Civilian Conservation Corps, Colorado and Wyoming District*.

Another history written a year or so later provides this effusive description of the camp: "Nestled back out of sight off the main road with a giant lateral moraine at its back door, a high ridge to the right, a pond, willow thicket and excellent fishing stream in the foreground, and distant, massive, impressive, spectacular Long's Peak literally in its front yard, is located Camp NP-4-C on Mill Creek. . . . The setting is excellent for a camp. The site is surrounded by more than fifty mountain peaks that raise their majestic heads above the 12,000-foot elevation mark. Wild life is abundant. Hundreds of deer and elk roam the hills daily. Beaver are common. Trout fishing is good."

Company 864 moved into large hospital tents erected on the site, where the ground had been leveled just enough to accommodate the tents, a bathhouse, and a mess hall—the latter two the only permanent buildings on the site. A few days later, fifty-four men arrived from Fort Logan, a few miles south of Colorado, and project superintendent M. J. Henry came to direct the company's activities in the park.

By the end of the summer, the army selected Camp NP-4-C to become a permanent campsite, making it necessary to build winter quarters. The army sent men to construct the buildings, and some of the men from Company 864 helped with this as well, but around October 1, the entire company was transferred to Phoenix, Arizona, making it certain that they would never know the pleasures of a winter in the heart of the Rocky Mountains.

"A standard camp consisted of about 20 to 30 structures that were usually arranged in a 'U' and usually included a recreation hall, garage, equipment maintenance building, hospital, administrative buildings and warehouse, officers quarters, mess hall and kitchen, lavatory and bath house, latrine, blacksmith shop, several barracks, technical service buildings, oil houses, pump house, generator house, and education buildings," Butler said in his report.

Two weeks after Company 864 departed, Company 1812 arrived from Grand Lake—and their first order of business involved digging the water line and plumbing for the new buildings, requiring them to break through frozen ground to dig a 4-foot-deep, 3,800-foot-long trench. Luckily, Company 1812's roster included a large majority of men from Colorado, so the perils of winter were nothing new to them. They made themselves at home at Camp NP-4-C for more than a year, and in addition to their assignments throughout the park, they landscaped the camp's grounds, built walkways, installed railings and steps, and made the site entirely comfortable until they departed in October of the following year.

In their place, a newly formed company of green recruits arrived: Company 2552, soon to be known as the Kentucky Gentlemen, as all of their number had just arrived from the green hills of that fair state. "They were very appreciative of the natural beauty they found surrounding them," notes a narrative written by on-site staff members L. A. Gleyre and C. N. Alleger in 1936. "They were pleased with the homelike atmosphere of the recreation hall and found it a center for winter activities."

CCC workers stayed in tents at Camp NP-4-C before they built permanent quarters in 1934. NATIONAL PARK SERVICE

Led by Lieutenant Wilburn E. Langlotz and Lieutenant Donald L. Cross, the Kentucky Gentlemen faced a hard Rocky Mountain winter, but they had the good sense to consider it a grand adventure. They made Thanksgiving and Christmas particularly special with huge roast turkeys, programs, and posing for a camp photo, and someone had the pleasure of playing Santa Claus and distributing gifts, candy, and nuts from the camp Christmas tree. "An election was held to determine the most representative enrollee in camp and Randall Bailey of Akron, Colorado, who is now Senior Leader, was chosen," the narrative tells us. "The Christmas menu was dedicated to him, his picture appeared on each copy."

The celebrations and recreational pursuits broke up a rigorous schedule of projects requiring the concentrated effort of body and mind, regardless of the season. Winter work involved removing and destroying old, unused roads, giving the trammeled land back to nature; some performed maintenance of the park's administrative buildings and grounds. In the winter of 1935–36, the men toiled diligently every workday but one, when the weather became too wintry to venture out.

"Perhaps one of the most important achievements of the CCC in this park was the control of a heavy infestation of Black Hills beetle in the Park Forests," notes the Gleyre and Alleger report. Park officials taught the men to recognize a tree that had been plundered by this destructive insect, and to cut down and burn these trees to remove the beetle from the park. "Every effort was made to eradicate completely this harmful forest insect, which not infrequently lays waste whole acres of valuable timber, and the park forests are once again free from serious infestation."

When they weren't hard at work on behalf of the park, the men spent the winter learning other skills they could take home with them and use to secure employment after their CCC term of enrollment. Listed among the instruction they could pursue were topics including "accounting, arithmetic, bookkeeping, conservation of natural resources, current events, dramatics, English, first aid, forestry, handicraft work, instrumental and vocal music, leaders' and assistant leaders' training, literacy, journalism, mechanical drawing, motion picture projection, nature hikes, photography, reading, safety, spelling, truck driving, typing, wild life conservation, and writing."

So eager were the men to learn that the corps commandeered rooms in the headquarters building, the mess halls, the recreation hall, an extra barracks building, and even private homes to accommodate everyone who wanted to take classes. "The educational work is very much a part of the enrollee's camp life," noted Gleyre and Alleger. Courses given by forestry and wildlife technicians were especially popular, as were photography developing and printing, woodworking, and a number of handicrafts. A report from Company 2552 noted that the men read 1,027 fiction books and 607 nonfiction books over the course of a year and attended more than sixty talks, including a dozen talks offered by the corps chaplains.

In addition to this well-rounded list of courses, most enrollees also received considerable vocational training. Instruction in auto mechanics, operation of heavy machinery, carpentry, concrete construction, sawmill operation, and truck driving culminated in a certificate the enrollee could take home and show to potential employers, confirming that he had received this specialized training.

In spring, the breadth and scope of the projects expanded, with CCC enrollees working throughout the park on endeavors that enhanced tourists' experience of the Rocky Mountains. They built trails, both to provide visitors with access to views and to clear the way for firefighters to pass into the backcountry; they improved and maintained campgrounds, and they constructed ponds in the park's fisheries to allow trout to grow to legal size before they were released into the park's lakes. As members of what many nicknamed Roosevelt's "tree army," they planted trees and shrubs where they had cleared out infested trees over the winter, reforesting the land and helping to prevent soil erosion. A number of the men became firefighters, ready at a moment's notice to assist in the suppression of a blaze anywhere in the park. Those with the appropriate skills even worked in the park offices and museums, providing assistance to rangers and others who had direct contact with the general public.

All of this activity made the enrollees' period in the park—each of them served from six months to two years—pass quickly, though not without some turmoil. With the distance of many decades between modern times and the years of the CCC, it can seem in hindsight that the corps existed in a bubble of order, goodwill, good works, and harmony.

Researcher Julia Brock, however, in a report to the park and the Rocky Mountain Nature Association in 2005, plumbed through camp newsletters, newspaper reports, and many other resources to determine what camp life was really like for the men in the CCC.

The new enrollees congregated at a training site before heading into the park for the first time; then they attended an orientation by the camp commander and received their package of supplies: "two pairs of shoes, three pairs of pants, two shirts, three changes of underwear, two jackets, overcoat caps, towels, toilet articles, blankets, sheets, cot, mattress, mess equipment, etc.," according to a 1937 annual report by the Colorado State Department of Public Welfare. They also received vaccines for typhoid fever and smallpox. The transition from their normal lives to the disciplined life of an army schedule suited some of the men just fine, but others balked at living under military regimentation.

The weekday began with reveille played by the camp bugler at 6:00 a.m. The men made their beds, straightened their barracks, ate breakfast at 7:00 a.m., and were out the door and on their way to their work projects by 8:00 a.m. They worked from 9:00 a.m. to noon, broke for lunch, and continued until 4:00 p.m., when they returned to their barracks, showered, and had supper at 5:00 p.m. After eating, the men had four hours to use as they pleased, taking courses, working on craft projects, playing sports, reading, participating in a camp orchestra or variety show rehearsal, or whatever else they chose. On weekends, the park provided transportation into town so the men could see movies, go to dances, or enjoy other activities in Estes Park or Grand Lake.

While the army supervised the camps, the men were not officially in the military, so they had the option of walking away if they found this regulated existence intolerable. Quite a number did leave, Brock discovered. "A few enrollees ultimately decided to abandon the camp even before their life in the Corps had begun," she said. "Many left only after a few weeks because of homesickness, something administrators tried to avoid by immediately starting the young men on Park work projects. . . . National statistics reported that as many as one out of five enrollees deserted until 1941, when the CCC began to curtail its operations because of the impending war."

In some cases, men who felt they were treated unfairly or that working conditions were too extreme attempted to take action to express their grievances. One of the most radical cases of this took place in Camp NP-4-C, when ninety men protested the treatment of truck drivers from their company. CCC administrators had commanded truck drivers to join the rest of the company in manual labor when they were not driving, and the truck drivers attempted to negotiate with administrators to keep from being forced to do this. The attempt to reach an agreement fell apart, however, and the army fired the drivers and discharged them from the CCC. This only fanned the flames of the camp's anger and the ninety men declared a strike, marched to the camp superintendent's home, and demanded that he speak to them. Soon army officers arrived, escorted the superintendent away from the scene, and quelled the uprising. And shortly thereafter, all ninety of the strikers received discharge papers.

More pervasive than protests over daily life, camp food, restrictions on leisure time, and other day-to-day grievances, however, were the issues involving race relations. Colorado's CCC camps were integrated, but only a few of the enrollees were black, and "racial discrimination was part of camp life," Brock said. Camp newsletters were "filled with racist jokes depicting blacks as backward and ignorant, as well as reporting the news of whole troupes of young men devoted to performing 'vodvil [*sic*] and minstrel' acts that centered on mocking African-American cultural lifeways."

Blacks were only one of the groups to encounter bigotry, Brock said: "White enrollees hurled slurs at men whose skin was any shade darker than theirs." Spanish Americans and Mexican immigrants finally had to be segregated from the white barracks throughout Colorado, though it isn't clear from the records if administrators in Rocky Mountain took this step. Camp newsletters have articles and letters from Spanish Americans drawing a line between themselves and Mexican immigrants, noting that the men of Spanish heritage were American citizens and should be treated as such. "This attitude was common in Spanish-American communities throughout Colorado, particularly in the northern part of the state; here the white-controlled, exploitive sugar-beet industry pitted migrant and native Chicanos against each other to compete for wage labor on farms," Brock explained. In 1939, in response to the racism Spanish-speaking men encountered throughout the state, the CCC began assigning these men "near communities that would accept them."

Overall, however, the men embraced the opportunity to become the image they had seen on the CCC's own literature before they enrolled: muscular men hardened by the outdoor life, the extraordinary landscape, and the challenging physical labor they performed every day. "Still today," Brock concludes, "the enrollee is depicted as a chiseled young man leaning confidently on his ax in the standard 'CCC Worker' statues that memorialize CCC sites across the nation."

REPURPOSING MORAINE PARK LODGE

Perhaps the most readily visible CCC project stands at Moraine Park. Long before it became part of a national park, Moraine Park was one of the most highly favored areas in the entire Rocky Mountain region of Colorado, with Eagle Cliff Mountain rising nearby, the magnificent view of the grassy meadow and the peaks that surround it, and the Big Thompson River ambling across the expanse. Most striking is the view of Longs Peak towering over Moraine Park's 8,100-foot elevation, with a margin of shrub-covered upland including gooseberry, common juniper, bitter brush, and ponderosa pine extending from the mountainside downward into the valley. Across the access road, a grove of aspens introduces another landscape element.

The setting has attracted visitors since the 1870s, with a number of these remaining to build homesteads and make the area their permanent or summer residence. Imogene Greene was one such tourist; so captivated was she by a visit to the Sprague Ranch in 1898, when she was fifty-four years old, that she built her own home here on a 160-acre parcel in 1903, naming the land Hillcrest. She married lumber dealer William D. MacPherson in 1905 and, as Imogene Greene MacPherson, she built a lodge on the property and went into business. She added a dining hall, guest cabins, and a livery stable, opening the resort and taking in her first paying guests in 1910 and soon gaining a reputation as a gracious hostess who made her guests comfortable and listened to their needs and suggestions. At the same time, she took a leadership role in the community, working alongside Enos Mills to make Rocky Mountain a national park.

Moraine Park had been a popular summer resort area before the Great Depression.
NATIONAL PARK SERVICE

After William's death in 1919, Mrs. MacPherson continued to operate the accommodations and keep them up-to-date with the latest amenities. Her advertising in 1920 declared, "Modern Improvements— Private Baths/Good Food And A Plenty," and noted that the lodge's own automobile would meet the stage in Estes Park and transport her guests to the resort. In October 1921, the *Estes Park Trail* reported that the lodge had added a new spring and a concrete tank for water storage, as "there are twenty-two baths connected with the Lodge's water system and during the heavy tourist season it has heretofore been taxed heavily."

Calling the lodge "The Resort That is Just Like Home" in her 1921 advertising, MacPherson set her cabin rates at nineteen to thirty-five dollars per week, or four to six dollars daily, including gas lighting, a tub and shower, and telephone and telegraph service. By this time, she had hired G. M. Derby to manage the property, as she herself was in her late seventies. Derby added an assembly and recreation hall in 1923, with dancing on the open second floor and a first-floor tearoom with its own fireplace, and opened it with "very elaborate ceremonies," including a costume ball with an orchestra. "Many of the costumes were exceedingly clever and some unusually unique," the *Estes Park Trail* said of the event, with prizes awarded for the best costumed gentleman, lady, and child. "The lighting effect in the hall was excellent and the spot light as it played on the various costumed dancers added much merriment to the occasion."

Mrs. MacPherson died in 1928, and her family took up the management of the lodge and its outbuildings, but the Great Depression significantly curtailed the flow of guests, and they soon understood that the economy made tourist travel a luxury people could no longer afford. The family did what Mother MacPherson probably would have done herself: They sold the property to the National Park Service in 1931, further supporting the park she helped to create. The MacPherson family netted $30,125 in the deal, a tidy sum for the time.

It was in Moraine Park Lodge's utility area that the first ECW company to arrive at Rocky Mountain National Park holed up until late spring snowstorms abated. Once the worst had passed and they erected the pyramidal tents for their summer camp, they began to deconstruct the resort. The park superintendent's monthly report of April 1933 detailed their tasks: "During the past month a crew of ECW men have been wrecking several of the old buildings. All material of value will be salvaged, the remainder is being given to people in the surrounding country for fire wood. When completed its obliteration will greatly improve the lower Moraine Park Valley." A month later, the next report noted, "The razing of the buildings at Moraine Lodge was finished and the crew was proceeding with filling up of the remaining excavations." By October, the work was just about complete, and the superintendent noted that twenty-seven buildings had been removed, "the earth regraded to its original slope and some planting done."

In 1936, with the resources and manpower of the CCC at its disposal, Rocky Mountain National Park turned the remaining Moraine Park Assembly Hall into a museum. They enclosed the lodge's open porch and stairs on either side of the building, installing small, single-light sash windows (which have since been replaced with picture windows). On the west side of the building, CCC workers "moved the first-story door a few feet southwest, to an existing window opening, and altered the original gable roof entry hood to a shed roof," the National Register of Historic Places official documents inform us. "On the southeast elevation, there was originally a small wing containing the kitchen, clad in shingles on

Converting an assembly hall in Moraine Park into a museum became a CCC project.
LIBRARY OF CONGRESS

the second floor and roofing paper on the first floor. The 1936 remodel changed the addition's exterior to a more compatible log veneer on the second floor and stone veneer on the first floor."

With these structural changes in place, the CCC made changes to the interior as well, converting the tearoom and dance hall into museum spaces. This included "placing exhibit cases against the exterior walls of the second floor and installing a large 'Indian Exhibit' in the center of the room," the National Register documents explain. "The old kitchen became an exhibit space for a 'Trapper's Cabin.'" Working closely with the park naturalist, CCC enrollees went on to build many of the museum exhibits.

Meanwhile, enrollees took on a project that required a great deal of new construction: the building of the Moraine Park Amphitheater. This new space would provide the park with an outdoor environment for

CCC crews built the Moraine Park Amphitheater as a place for tourists to learn about the park and interact with rangers. NATIONAL PARK SERVICE

presentations, films, ranger talks, and other opportunities to educate the general public about the park and its many resources, broadening and enhancing tourists' experience of visiting the park.

"Important built features include ... plank and stone seating, drainage structures, the foundation of the [projection] screen, and fire pit; pedestrian circulations system including stone steps and trails; and the entry road and parking lot, including stone culverts," National Register documents noted. A natural stand of ponderosa pine trees formed a dark, dramatic backdrop behind the wooden projection screen, a second benefit beyond the area's natural bowl-shape, making it an ideal spot for a presentation space. Here rangers would offer education programs using the leading-edge projection technology of the time: lantern slides, consisting of painted or photographic pictures on glass plates, projected by a concave mirror behind a light source onto a lens in the front of the projector. "Magic" lantern technology, as it had been known since the nineteenth century, served presenters well until the much less cumbersome 35-millimeter slide projector technology emerged in the 1950s.

The CCC crew began the project by removing all of the other buildings erected by the MacPhersons—again, a total of twenty-seven structures, including the guest cabins, dining hall, and stable—to return the land to its wild state. Work then began on the amphitheater, with a design that called for the use of native plants and materials to blend the space into the existing landscape as seamlessly as possible. "The basic tenets of this NPS naturalistic design was that architecture would play a subordinate role to nature, the massing of the structure would respond to the terrain, and the design would hide and blend with the naturalness of the setting," the National Register documents explained. "The use of native material available in the vicinity of the site was encouraged, making stone and timber the materials of choice for most parks, including Rocky Mountain National Park."

The designer drew on the example set in Yosemite National Park, where the Park Service's first woodland amphitheater provided "a rustic interpretation of the Greek amphitheater built into a hillside with seating radiating in semicircles from a center stage." The Moraine Park Amphitheater became the standard for such structures, as the Park Service's 1938 architectural style manual noted two years later.

Construction began on April 25, 1936, according to park records. Using wood drawn from the park for plank seating and stone foundations for the planks, the CCC constructed a ring with sixteen rows of seats in two arcs, ascending upward in steps along the sides of the natural earthen bowl. "The seats sit on somewhat regular stones some 10" high," the park's Cultural Landscapes Inventory (CLI) document explains. "Concrete mortar stabilizes the rocks holding the rectangular seating planks. Timber wedges (11" × 4") lie on these stone walls about 4–5 feet apart, with rectangular planks of milled lumber (2¼" × 11" × 4–6") nailed to the wedges. The joinery between the planks as well as the wedges use large unfinished nails." The seating in one area accommodates an existing tree, forming a planting bed around it. On the ground in the center, a fire pit preceded a cement slab that held a projection booth for both still and moving pictures, and a solid wooden screen on a stand.

The main body of the project came to its conclusion in late summer, and by the first days of fall, the crew had moved on to construction of the parking area, moving 560 cubic yards of dirt to create the lot. Work ended in October when Company 2552's time in Rocky Mountain came to an end. The Kentucky Gentlemen had been recalled to their home state back in April, so it was seventy-four men from Ohio who did the work in Moraine Lake throughout the spring and summer—and in October 1936, they, too, headed for home ready to seek employment using their new skills.

Company 3884 arrived at Camp NP-4-C on October 18, 1936, under the command of Lieutenant W. J. Magill and Second Lieutenant William Musgrave, just in time to spend the winter there. These men hailed mostly from Colorado, with some arriving from Texas, Arizona, Missouri, and Arkansas, and a few may have been about to experience the first winter of their lives. They settled in for what they expected to be a rugged but comfortable season, but fate had other ideas: the arrival of a particularly frigid winter froze all of the water lines to the camp, forcing the army's technical service crew to haul in water "for all uses in the camp" for a grueling four months. "But the program of the camp went on as usual," the official report said, "which speaks very highly of the personnel and the members of this company. Hardships were endured during this very cold winter, at which the boys laugh now, which shows more than anything else the spirit of the CCC."

The final work on the Moraine Park amphitheater came in May 1937, as Company 3884 picked up where Company 2552 left off the previous fall. CCC men built a trail and steps to the amphitheater, as well as the path to the museum, the surface of the parking area, and a complex erosion control system to complete the project.

"Numerous stone drainage structures move water through the site," the CLI said. "Drainage features include a 60-foot-long stone gutter above the amphitheater, which channels water into a drain. A steel drain grate lies behind the screen foundation at the edge of the stage area. At the bottom of the slope below the stage area, a 24-inch steel culvert with stone and concrete battlements channels water under the entry road. Down the slope from this culvert, lies another stone battlement and culvert that carries water under Bear Lake Road. To the southeast, a second system of matching stone battlements and steel culverts moves water under the roads. This drainage pattern points to the elaborate construction techniques used in the creation of the site."

The amphitheater opened to the public for the first time on August 6, 1937, with ninety-seven people in attendance, "a very encouraging prospect for the new centralized lecture program," the Superintendent's Report for July 1937 said. It went on to note that audiences remained steady: "Development of the new lecture center at Moraine Park Amphitheatre has shown itself to be logical, in that attendance has been showing a steady figure of from 75 to 100 when weather conditions are favorable. Rainy and cold evenings out crowds somewhat, but no lectures are postponed, rather being held inside the museum in improvised arrangements."

TRAILS, CAMPGROUNDS, AND FISHERIES

Today visitors to Rocky Mountain who leave their vehicles to explore beyond the roads may find themselves on a trail constructed or improved by CCC crews. In 1932, the year before the CCC arrived, the park had about two hundred miles of trails already in place, an increase of more than seventy miles since the land became a national park in 1915. By the time the CCC left the park in 1941, just about one hundred miles of additional trails had been built—some by park trail crews, but most by the enrollees.

Because of changes in nomenclature and directional cues over the decades, it's not always clear which trails the CCC crews built or improved, but we know that they cleared and graded fire trails that became the Red Mountain, Colorado River, and Columbine Creek trails now used by thousands of tourists annually. A foot trail from Glacier Basin to the YMCA in Estes Park was an early priority, and others included the construction of bridges over streams, opening areas of the park to hikers that had been inaccessible before.

One of these, the Twin Sisters trail, provides a 7.5-mile out-and-back hike to the top of a mountain ridge with unbeatable views of the mountains from Twin Sisters Peak. While CCC members generally worked on lower elevation trails where they could be supplied with food, water, and medical supplies with ease, this trail begins at 9,040 feet and climbs nearly 2,500 feet to 11,428 feet, where trees are replaced by a talus slope just about 300 feet above tree line—a point where daily windy conditions and loose rock slabs would have made the work particularly challenging.

Improving campgrounds became an important priority for the park in the 1930s. The park had five campgrounds at the time, and three of them—Endovalley, Aspenglen, and Glacier Basin—had emerged as the most in demand with tourists. Work began at these campgrounds with the creation of boundaries around parking areas and individual campsites, using large rocks and logs to protect the land beyond each site, in the interest of maintaining the natural surroundings and native plants. Brick fireplaces for cooking and combination tables and benches came next, making each site more comfortable for tent camping; later, when visitors started to arrive more frequently with camper trailers in tow, CCC workers added water and comfort stations in each campground.

Today fishing is a carefully regulated sport in Rocky Mountain with an emphasis on preserving the park's two native trout species—the greenback cutthroat and the Colorado River cutthroat—but in the 1930s, the US Bureau of Fisheries established a policy that encouraged stocking of park waters with several different native and nonnative fish species. Lower-elevation rivers and lakes in the park had long been celebrated as prime fishing areas, with the added pleasures of glorious scenery and peaceful surroundings, so attracting more anglers with well-stocked waterways became a high priority. CCC enrollees were tasked with the construction of four breeding ponds to produce enough trout for all of the park's eligible waters, placing them in Horseshoe Park and Holowell Park, on the east side of the Continental Divide, and near the Endovalley campground and not far from Grand Lake, on the western side.

These 210-foot-long, 100-foot-wide ponds were each ten feet deep. Creating space for these large breeding ponds involved a crew of thirty-five men to clear the land of its trees and woodland detritus and then build a clay dike and a large basin made of concrete. Water arrived in the basin from an intake dam, piped in from beneath the structure. With the pond completed and filled, CCC enrollees went to the Estes Park hatchery and gathered trout fry to transfer into the pond. Months later, when the fry were large enough, the enrollees gathered the fully grown fish once again and toted them to the nearby lake or river to release them there.

The stocking program continued in the park until 1969, when attitudes changed about bringing nonnative Yellowstone cutthroat trout into the park's waterways because of their effect on native fish populations. Today only forty-eight of the 156 lakes in the park sustain their own reproducing fish, as the other lakes are at high elevations where the water is too cold and the habitat is too rugged for spawning. The park still stocks the lower lakes but only to restore the two trout species native to the park.

The CCC's impact on Rocky Mountain cannot be overstated, from the removal and repurposing of old structures to soil erosion control and eradication of destructive insects. By 1941, it seemed that the corps's role in the National Park Service system could continue indefinitely . . . but the Japanese attack on Pearl Harbor on December 7, 1941, created a dramatic need for able-bodied soldiers, and the US Army moved quickly to draft CCC enrollees, members of current companies as well as those who had moved on. Many of these men received the rank of corporal or sergeant in recognition of their training in parks and other national areas across the country, providing the armed forces with a roster of men who could assist with command from their first day in the army.

The war signaled the end of the CCC, but its imprint remains in thousands of parks across the country. Today we look back on what seemed to be an idyllic notion: the concept of hundreds of thousands of men working together for the betterment of our natural spaces—and while it had its faults, this effort generated public works that park visitors will enjoy for many generations to come.

Returning to Nature

*Said tract is dedicated and set apart as a public park for the benefit
and enjoyment of the people of the United States, under the name of
the Rocky Mountain National Park . . . with regulations being primarily aimed at the freest use of the said park for recreation purposes
by the public and for the preservation of the natural conditions and
scenic beauties thereof.*
> —Sixty-third Congress of the United States,
> Session III, Chapter 19
> January 25, 1915

What do people remember most about their visit to Rocky Mountain National Park? Visitors may have a wide variety of answers to this question—a favorite hike, a horseback ride along a trail, a climb to the top of Longs Peak or Mount Meeker, an encounter with bighorn sheep or bugling elk, or a drive along Fall River Road—but one feature underlies them all and unites tourists in the same impression. It's the landscape, of course, the vast views and mountain vistas that make Rocky Mountain distinctly different from all others. Many national parks in the western states have mountains, but few rival the quantity, variety, and height of these peaks or the arcs they form through so much of the park's nearly 415 square miles.

When this land became a national park in 1915, however, the sweeping views had more in them than grassy valleys and craggy peaks. The Homestead Act of 1862 had brought thousands of people into these 265,000-plus acres, dividing up the land into 160-acre patches and filling them with cabins, barns, sheds, and all kinds of other structures. Other sections, also within the magic 160-acre measurements, contained large, 10-foot-deep holes in the ground where shafts had been dug in the search for gold and silver; some of these continued well beyond the initial dig if the lode looked promising. Enos Mills and his colleagues saw the potential of this expansive area to provide peace, solitude, and thrilling vistas to visitors, but they had not put forth any specific plan for restoring the land to wilderness once the federal government had officially acquired it.

Was restoration necessary? According to the National Park Service, it was part of the job of every national park. "The guiding principle followed is that the natural conditions of the parks must be disturbed as little as possible consistent with necessary development in the public interest, and where such conditions have been unnecessarily or carelessly or wrongfully changed in the past they must be restored where this can be done, and in any case made less objectionable if restoration to a state of nature is impossible," NPS director Stephen Mather wrote in his report to the secretary of the interior in 1919. "This principle is a corollary of the governing rule in our general policy that 'the national parks must be maintained in absolutely unimpaired form for the use of future generations as well as those of our own time.'"

So many structures within the newly established park, however, posed a knottier problem than many other national parks faced at the time of their formation. The process to resolve this issue in Rocky Mountain spanned decades. Incremental gains came in spurts of activity, some of it driven by larger government programs and some by careful research, involvement of the National Register of Historic Places, and individual researchers from area colleges and universities. Questions had to be answered about each property's historical value, its safety for visitors and staff, and whether it represented an opportunity to teach or to remind tourists of a tale that would otherwise be lost to the passage of time. In addition, some structures had sentimental value to families, as well as property value that might net them a tidy sum from the federal government.

The National Park Service trod cautiously as it addressed the question of previously inhabited lands, and in the process removed hundreds of structures. Today we enjoy a vast landscape of untrammeled mountains, valleys, meadows, and waterways, with hundreds of miles of trails to take us into the wilds of the Rockies.

Getting to this point, however, was not an easy journey, and that journey is still in progress.

NOT YOUR GRANDFATHER'S NATIONAL PARK

"When [Rocky Mountain National Park] was established, various management plans were adopted but in general, the pre-existing inholdings were allowed to continue operations, especially as they related to serving visitors to the park," wrote Barb Boyer Buck of the *Estes Park Trail-Gazette* in 2015. "In the 1930s, the park's philosophy shifted to one of restoring the park land to its natural state and [the National Park Service] began purchasing the private land whenever it could. When it did, the existing buildings were in most cases dismantled."

The Holzwarth ranch, for example, remained in operation as a guest accommodation until the early 1970s. Moraine Park, a settlement on the northeastern side of the park, continued to serve residents and about four hundred guests every summer until 1931 with a number of amenities that included a post office, a grocery store, lodges, working farmland, and a golf course.

"Today at Moraine Park, we see only a fraction of the buildings that once populated the area," Buck continued. The cabin that belonged to Pulitzer Prize–winning journalist William Allen White is now a historic site, and an assembly hall became the Moraine Park Museum (see the previous chapter). "But the Brinwood [Hotel and Ranch], Moraine Lodge, and most significantly, the original homestead of Abner Sprague, established in 1875 and grown over the years to include 600 acres on which sat 30 buildings (including several lodge buildings), grazing fields, and the golf course, was purchased and all buildings were removed." The National Park Service paid $750,000 for this land in 1962.

Reclamation of the land within the park's boundaries was part of the plan for Rocky Mountain from the beginning, and no one expected this to happen overnight. Residents who had family lands that had become part of the national park received a solid offer from the National Park

Service: full rights to the land as long as the owners kept it within the family, passing it to their descendants over as many generations as they wished. When the family decided it was time to sell, the park bought their land at fair market value. "The park is not going anywhere, and is capable of waiting a long time," a park chief engineer told Shawn Habecker, a researcher who studied the building removal process in 1994. After the final purchase of the property, the park could make a determination about the buildings standing on the land: If they had a historical story to tell, or if they could be of use to the Park Service as offices, visitor centers, or museums, they might be preserved; if they were structurally unstable and needed to be removed for purposes of public safety, if they had no historic value, or if the landscape would be improved by their removal, they were razed.

For fourteen years after the dedication of Rocky Mountain National Park, existing lodges and other guest accommodations operated within the park, creating any number of delightful experiences for guests. Then, nearly overnight, changes took place across the country that would require a new approach to these buildings, as their owners found themselves unable to sustain the businesses they had worked so hard to build.

THE CRASH, THE CORPS, AND THE WAR

The stock market crash in October 1929 and the subsequent Great Depression brought cataclysmic change to American families, wiping out the discretionary income that had allowed average folks to take nice vacations. With 25 percent of able-bodied workers unemployed and long lines at shelters for meal handouts, the number of people who could consider a trip to the western national parks dropped dramatically. Remarkably, Rocky Mountain National Park not only maintained its annual visitation numbers during the Depression but also increased them. Lodges like Moraine, Brinwood, and many others did not see the benefits of this tourist activity, however, as visitors sought less expensive alternatives to these accommodations. Many of the once-popular lodges went out of business.

The park saw one major benefit during this difficult time, however: the arrival of the CCC, coinciding with the need to begin to remove aging and abandoned structures from inside the park boundaries, an endeavor described in the previous chapter. The CCC removed twenty-seven structures from Moraine Park alone, as well as disused roads that led to scattered settlements in other areas of the park, and buildings that remained in these settlements. Many of these had already deteriorated significantly over time, especially those that had been left to their own devices for decades either by homesteaders who had given up on Colorado after a few rough winters or by miners who did not find the fortune they sought in the 1850s or 1890s.

"Concern for the harmonization of construction and nature led park designers to adapt principles of natural landscape design for restoring building sites to a natural condition after construction," wrote Linda Flint McClelland in her book, *Presenting Nature: The Historic Landscape Design of the National Park Service 1916 to 1942*. "Plantings erased the lines between the earth and manmade structures, returned construction sites to their natural condition, and overall enhanced the natural beauty of the parks. Landscape naturalization included the beautification of park entrances and villages, vista clearing, the development of overlooks, the rehabilitation of springs and streams, and 'cleanup' projects to remove fallen timber and snags or to restore areas damaged by flood, fire, or blight." Crews transplanted shrubs and other native plants into disturbed areas after buildings were removed. They also added new saplings to start the growth of native trees, one method designers used to "erase the scars of construction and control pedestrian and automobile traffic in heavily visited areas."

The CCC conducted extensive cleanup activities around the mines themselves as well, clearing out discarded shovels, picks, drills, wheelbarrows, ore cars and tracks, and other detritus left behind by discouraged prospectors. (Later, in the 1960s, the Mineral Mining Service established an Abandoned Mine program to close and fill in the dangerous holes in the ground left by these mining operations, sealing the shafts with steel bars or "collapsing the entrances," according to a report by park archaeologist William Butler in 2006.)

"There are over seven hundred razed structures listed in the files of the Rocky Mountain National Park," Habecker noted at the end of his study. "Some of them were used until the upkeep became overwhelming and [they] were then destroyed. . . . They ranged in size from sixty-room lodges to one-hole privies." Some of these were constructed by the Park Service for specific purposes, but they succumbed to the elements or they could not withstand topographical issues like erosion. Others had no practical or historical purpose once the owner had moved on.

When the Japanese attacked Pearl Harbor on December 7, 1941, and America declared war on Japan on December 8, the United States focused entirely on supporting the war effort and mobilizing to protect itself and win overseas. World War II meant that families stopped taking vacations altogether, as more than sixteen million Americans enlisted or were drafted to serve in the military. Park rangers were called to active duty, and 1,200 employees—nearly 20 percent of its total workforce—left the National Park Service for the military. The Park Service had swelled by then to include 164 parks, historic sites, monuments, battlefields, recreation areas, rivers, and seashores, and it faced enormous pressure to open the lands it preserved to logging, mining, and grazing of livestock to supply the war effort.

"Requests ranged from demands to melt Civil War cannons and statuary for scrap metal to logging virgin stands of trees," a report on the National Park Service website said. "For the duration of the war, Secretary of the Interior Harold Ickes, National Park Service Director Newton Drury, and park employees struggled to balance unwavering support of the war effort with their mission to protect park resources for future generations."

At the same time, visitation across all of the national parks reached its lowest point since the creation of the National Park Service. Rocky Mountain had reached the highest visitation in its existence in 1941, with 681,845 visitors, but by 1943, visitors had dwindled to 124,353—a drop of 82 percent. With proprietors going off to war and no one coming to the park, hospitality businesses within the park closed their doors. Over time, the remaining buildings fell into disrepair.

Mission 66

After the war, Americans returning from overseas found jobs, built homes, and began to prosper, and visitors came back to Rocky Mountain in droves, bringing their families in cars and finding accommodations in

Estes Park and Grand Lake. Parks across the country had suffered during the war, however, as funding had been cut to the bone and even basic maintenance had become impossible with limited staff and no resources.

"Rocky's rangers could not keep up with the demands of growing problems such as highway and backcountry accidents, vandalism (including removal of signs and roof shingles for campfire wood), excessive littering at campgrounds and roadsides, and lack of sanitary facilities," said a report by the Colorado State University (CSU) Public Lands History Center. "As a result of the wartime and postwar budgetary constraints, the park constructed only two entirely new buildings between 1939 and 1956: an employee's washhouse . . . on Sundance Circle and the Hidden Valley Lodge. However, Rocky began to make use of the former CCC buildings and those acquired from purchased inholdings." The park moved entire buildings from CCC camps and former guesthouses to employee residential areas within the park, providing seasonal housing for its rangers and maintenance staff. This, however, only served as a stopgap measure. "The long list of backlogged facility needs demanded new structures," the CSU report noted.

At the same time, the way people used the parks had changed as well. Now every family had a car, so visitors had ready transportation when they arrived at the park, and they could go into and come out of the park at will. They wanted to drive through and admire the scenery, stop for a short while at the most spectacular views, park, enjoy a day hike, and go on to the next wonderful place. The promise of a new interstate highway system, President Dwight D. Eisenhower's crowning achievement, would allow visitors to travel quickly between America's scenic wonders and cover hundreds of miles in a single trip, so by completion of the first stretches of highway in the 1960s, the length of their stay in one park would decrease even further. Camping often involved trailers or tents packed into the back of a station wagon, which needed to be parked at a campsite not far from a road. Instead of sprawling lodges and quaint cabins inside the park, these visitors needed restrooms and a place to connect with a ranger to gather basic information about what they could see in a day or less.

The world had changed, and the parks had to keep up. National Park Service director Conrad Wirth managed to convince Eisenhower and his cabinet to provide a decade of funding for his brainchild: Mission 66, a plan to prepare for the fiftieth anniversary of the National Park Service in 1966 by completing a decade of construction projects, including roads, trails, and thousands of facilities throughout the park system. This massive undertaking would bring the parks, which Director Drury had called "victims of the war," into the latter half of the twentieth century by protecting natural resources and creating an extraordinary visitor experience.

In Rocky Mountain, park superintendent James V. Lloyd asked the staff to "think big," according to the CSU report, as if they were planning the park from scratch. "Outmoded facilities will be replaced with physical improvements adequate for expected demands but so designed and located as to reduce the impact of public use on valuable and destructible features," the resulting prospectus stated. To accomplish this, the park requested more than ten million dollars: nine million to go to the park and a little more than one million to be used for improvements to the Shadow Mountain Recreation Area, which the park managed.

Planning and construction began almost immediately. The Beaver Meadows entrance station opened in 1960, and the Alpine Visitor Center at Fall River Pass opened on July 16, 1965, the same day that the park broke ground on a new administration building at Beaver Meadows. Funding continued through the 1960s and allowed the park to complete another headquarters, the West Side Administration Building—what we now know as the Kawuneeche Visitor Center—on the other side of the park at Grand Lake. At the same time, the park's Mission 66 plan involved "increased efforts to acquire inholdings, remove old buildings, and restore the natural landscape as much as possible," according to *Mission 66 Visitor Centers: The History of a Building Type*, by Sarah Allaback.

Through this initiative, the park bought Fern Lake Lodge, Bear Lake Lodge, the Sprague Lodges, the Fall River Lodge in Horseshoe Park, the Brinwood Hotel, and the Stead Ranch at Moraine Park, where an Estes Park favorite, the Deer Ridge Chalet, had stood for decades. The focus on the parks' environment over guest accommodations and other forms of development had taken hold across the country, as Mission 66 redirected management plans to fulfill their original purpose. "For visitors to Rocky Mountain National Park, this transition is most visible today in

Spragues Lodge, one of the oldest accommodations in the area, stood in Moraine Park. NATIONAL PARK SERVICE

the park's concentrated front country campgrounds and picnic areas, the modern improvements along Trail Ridge Road[,] . . . the entrance roads into the park, and in the three unique, yet related, visitor centers in the Mission 66 Park Service Modern style," said a report by the Colorado State University Public Lands History Center.

"The idea was to make the park an outdoor museum," one that "could be toured and viewed primarily from your car," wrote Barb Boyer Buck in a 2015 article for the *Estes Park Trail Gazette*. Replacing the unique architecture of Rocky Mountain's old lodges with new, modern visitor centers did not sit well with many longtime residents of Estes Park, however. "While some of the criticism of Mission 66 surrounded the utilitarian architecture used for its buildings, in Estes Park the dismay centered around the razing of historic sites and lodges, forever changing the way people visited and obliterating examples of the area's homesteading heritage. . . . This architectural style, named Rocky Mountain Rustic or Rocky Mountain Stick, was a combination of Victorian and Adirondack styles—with decorative embellishments created with unpainted, unplaned tree logs and twigs. In many cases, the twisting pine character of the wood was retained and incorporated into the design."

News of the elimination of these lodges pushed the Estes Park Chamber of Commerce and the Town of Estes Park into demanding a review of the park's policy regarding demolition of buildings, which apparently led to some confrontations between town officials, landowners of the park's inholdings, and Superintendent Lloyd. These landowners felt that Lloyd was trying to force them out of the park—but others who completed land transactions with the park felt they had been treated equitably and did not join the protest. Enough vitriol came to the surface, however, that the park considered leaving two lodges intact: Fall River Lodge, in Horseshoe Park, and the Brinwood Hotel, in Moraine Park. The park already owned the Brinwood and had placed it in the hands of a concessionaire in 1932, so staff looked into finding new management for the property. "But the cost of the required renovations discouraged bidders," the CSU report said. "Both closed in 1959 and the park restored the sites to natural conditions."

It also didn't help that in 1955, the park had built a ski facility at Hidden Valley, where skiing had taken place on an ad hoc basis for decades. It seemed to many area residents to have run counter to the park's commitment to the restoration of the natural environment. (Hidden Valley closed to skiing in 1991, and the park razed the lodge in 2002.)

Looking for a way to ease tensions with Estes Park, park administration and architect Edmund Thomas Casey of Taliesin Associates Architects worked closely with town officials to place the new Beaver Meadows Visitor Center in the town, just outside of the park entrance. Superintendent Granville B. Liles, "with perhaps a greater sense of diplomacy than former Superintendent Lloyd," according to the CSU report, "hoped its accessible location outside of the park's entrance fee station would provide an opportunity to improve Rocky's relationship with the Estes Park residents."

Indeed, the *Estes Park Trail* noted in September 1964 that the park had chosen a site "such that it will serve visitors of the Estes Park area without requiring them to enter the National Park itself." Today the location allows people to visit the facility's restaurant, large gift shop, and information center without paying a fee to enter the park, making it a meeting place for residents as well as tourists.

As controversial as it was at the time, the decision to remove these lodges and guest cabins in the park did lead to a boom of hotel construction in the park's entrance towns, turning them both into popular resort areas and greatly expanding the tourism industry at both ends of the park. "Estes Park and Grand Lake depended on park-related tourism even before Mission 66 began," said the CSU report. "Mission 66 planners expected the gateway towns to expand and provide services that park villages inside the boundaries had formerly provided. But they failed to anticipate the controversy of removing existing structures and the local nostalgia for historic lodges. In Rocky's case, building removal within the park had been in the works for years as park managers sought to restore 'natural conditions.'"

Not all of the old lodges ended up as heaps of scrap wood. Bear Lake Lodge, once a popular spot for overnight accommodations and a boys' camp, was scheduled for demolition in 1959 and 1960, but part of it received a last-minute reprieve when the Rimrock Company purchased the Upper Bear Lake Lodge building in 1966. The new owners carefully

Deer Ridge Chalet was one of the most popular landmarks in the park.
NATIONAL PARK SERVICE

dismantled it and moved it to what is now the Elk Meadow Lodge and RV Resort in Estes Park, where it still serves visitors today. The rest of the buildings were demolished, and a dense forest now covers the area.

Deer Ridge Lodge, one of the most beloved buildings in the park by the locals, came up for demolition just as the Estes Park Lodge of Masons #183 determined that they needed a permanent building instead of meeting in the Estes Park Golf and Country Club Pro Shop. "The forces of destiny joined company in 1960 when Rocky Mountain National Park began condemnation proceedings to obtain possession of Deer Ridge Enterprises and the need of Estes Park Lodge #183 to proceed with plan to build, or otherwise obtain, a lodge building of their own," the Masonic Lodge's website explains. "The Members of the Masonic foundation turned their thoughts towards joining together the existing, large portions of the Deer Ridge buildings into one composite structure." Working with the Denver architectural firm Muchow & Associates, the Masons combined five structures from the Deer Ridge property and dedicated the finished building in September 1963. Today it remains a distinguished landmark and event center on South St. Vrain Avenue.

Visitors today enjoy wide nature views because of an ongoing effort to remove buildings and restore the landscape. MACKENZIE REED, NATIONAL PARK SERVICE

The acquisition of privately owned land over the last century has created a pristine national park. MACKENZIE REED, NATIONAL PARK SERVICE

Beyond the restoration of wilderness landscapes and the construction of new visitor centers and other facilities, Mission 66 resulted in many improvements in park infrastructure that most visitors either took for granted or were altogether unaware of. Housing for more than 150 staff members, using standardized templates in the new Park Service Modern style, sprang up on the east side of the park, at the Grand Lake and Fall River entrances, and in Hidden Valley and Wild Basin. New water and sewer systems allowed the park to bring flush toilets into its visitor centers and campgrounds, and water treatment facilities made certain that the park's water supply was free of contaminants. Electricity powered lights at campgrounds for the first time. Restrooms, utility buildings, and ranger stations took on the standardized style we now recognize throughout parks across the country, using "low, horizontal profiles, stone veneers, wood siding, and dark or muted paint colors," as the CSU report describes them. "Standardization of design ensured that campers in any park knew the nearest comfort station or ranger kiosk."

The effects of this period of reimagination in the national parks continue today, but now these elements have become such a part of the park experience that visitors expect them to stay in keeping with "national park standards." In 1973, with the establishment of new definitions of wilderness areas in the parks, the focus shifted once again, this time to preserving nature without allowing the further invasion of buildings and roads. The removal of buildings in Rocky Mountain continued with the razing of the Hidden Valley ski facilities, emergency housing and other structures installed by the Park Service in the 1950s, and miscellaneous others, but the greater efforts have gone into restoring nature where evidence of human habitation still lingers.

Forests and meadows now grace the land where settlements and homesteads once stood, and individual historic sites tell the stories of an era when the cry of "Free land!" meant prosperity for a lucky few. Rocky Mountain National Park now draws more than 4.4 million people annually. They come to see the unspoiled landscapes and marvel at the work of nature, perhaps never knowing that it was human intervention that kept these vistas pure.

References

The First Inhabitants

Benedict, James B. Prehistoric Man and Environment in the High Colorado Mountains: A Progress Report on Field Work During the Summer of 1969 Under National Science Foundation Grant GS-2606. National Science Foundation, 1969.

Benedict, James B. "The Murray Site: A Late Prehistoric Game Drive System in the Colorado Rocky Mountains." *Plains Anthropologist*, Vol. 20, No. 69, August 1975, pp. 161–174.

Benedict, James B. "Footprints in the Snow: High-Altitude Cultural Ecology of the Colorado Front Range, USA." *Arctic and Alpine Research*, Vol. 24, No. 1, 1992, pp. 1–16.

Benedict, James B. "Archaeologists Above Timberline: The Early Years." *Southwestern Lore*, Vol. 67, No. 2, Summer 2001, pp. 1–16.

Benedict, James B., Benedict, Robert J., Lee, Craig M., and Staley, Dennis M. "Spruce Trees from a Melting Ice Patch: Evidence for Holocene Climatic Change in the Colorado Rocky Mountains, USA." *The Holocene*, Vol. 18, No. 7, November 2008, pp. 1067–1076.

Brunswig, Robert H. Prehistoric, Protohistoric, and Early Historic Native American Archaeology of Rocky Mountain National Park: Volume 1—Final Report of Systemwide Archaeological Inventory Program Investigations by the University of Northern Colorado (1998–2002). National Park Service, Rocky Mountain National Park, 2005.

Butler, William B. Rocky Mountain National Park Research Design for Archaeology. Rocky Mountain National Park, 1997.

Husted, Wilfred M. "Prehistoric Occupation of the Alpine Zone in the Rocky Mountains." *Arctic and Alpine Environments*, eds. Jack D. Ives and Roger G. Barry. Methuen, London, 1974, p. 865.

Ives, Ronald L. "Early Human Occupation of the Colorado Headwaters Region: An Archaeological Reconnaissance." *Geographical Review*, Vol. 32, No. 3, July 1942, pp. 448–462. https://www.jstor.org/stable/210387?seq=1#page_scan_tab_contents.

Lee, Craig M., and Benedict, James B. "Ice Bison, Frozen Forests, and the Search for Archaeology in Colorado Front Range Ice Patches." *Colorado Archaeology*, Vol. 78, No. 1, Spring 2012, pp. 41–46.

Mead, J. R. "Ancient Stone Remains on Summit of Rocky Mountains." Paper reprinted in the *Kansas City Review of Science and Industry*, Vol. 5, 1882.

Morris, Elizabeth. "Prehistoric Game Drive System in the Rocky Mountains and High Plains Areas of Colorado." *Hunters of the Recent Past*, eds. Leslie B. Davis and Brian O. K. Reeves. Routledge, London, 2014, pp. 195–207. https://books.google .com/books?id=iRkhBQAAQBAJ&pg=PA207&lpg=PA207&dq=Archaeological +Survey+of+Rocky+Mountain+National+Park+Yelm&source=bl&ots=w_mk0T9 DxS&sig=NO7hZgCOop2cNR3o3_46Q6YgafQ&hl=en&sa=X&ved=2ahUKE wj-t_Tljc3eAhUR24MKHd4FDE4Q6AEwBHoECAYQAQ#v=onepage&q =Yelm&f=false.

Pitblado, Bonnie L., and Brunswig, Robert H. *That Was Then, This Is Now: Seventy-Five Years of Paleoindian Research in Colorado*. Frontiers in Colorado Paleoindian Archaeology. University Press of Colorado, Boulder, 2007.

Sprague, A. E. "Prehistoric Trails." *Estes Park Trail*, August 1, 1930, p. 20.

Van Elsacker, Diana. "Evaluation: High Altitude Game Drive Complexes Along the Front Range Crest, Rollins Pass Site." Paper written for History 685, Historic Preservation, University of Colorado, November 8, 1978.

The Ute and the Arapaho

Beals, Ralph L. *Ethnology of Rocky Mountain National Park: The Ute and the Arapaho*. National Park Service, US Department of the Interior, 1936.

Brunswig, Robert H. "Apachean Archaeology of Rocky Mountain National Park, Colorado, and the Colorado Front Range." *From the Land of Ever Winter to the American Southwest: Athapaskan Migrations, Mobility, and Ethnogenesis*, ed. Deni J. Seymour, University of Utah Press, Salt Lake City, 2012, pp. 20–36.

Brunswig, Robert H., McBeth, Sally, and Elinoff, Louise. "Re-Enfranchising Native Peoples in the Southern Rocky Mountains: Integrated Contributions of Archaeo-logical and Ethnographic Studies on Federal Lands." *Post-Colonial Perspectives in Archaeology*, eds. Peter Bikoulis, D. Lacroix, and M. Peuramaki-Brown. Chacmool Archaeological Association, Calgary, Canada, 2010, pp. 55–69.

Butler, W. *Indian Names in Rocky Mountain National Park*. Rocky Mountain National Park, 2008.

Cowell, Andrew. "Arapaho Creation Story." Wyoming Legends. Accessed November 12, 2018. https://wyominglegends.wordpress.com/2014/10/25/arapaho-creation-story.

Duncan, Clifford H, and Goss, James A. *Consultation on Traditional Ute Sites in Rocky Mountain National Park, August 22, 23, and 24, 2000*. Ute Indian Tribe of Utah and Texas Tech University, 2000.

McBeth, Sally. Native American Oral History and Cultural Interpretation in Rocky Mountain National Park. University of Northern Colorado, Greeley, 2007.

Toll, Oliver W. *Arapaho Names & Trails: A Report of a 1914 Pack Trip*. Rocky Mountain Nature Association, Estes Park, CO, 1962, 2003.

Ute Mountain Ute Cultural Affairs Office. "Creation Story—Senawahv's People." His-tory Colorado. Accessed November 13, 2018. http://exhibits.historycolorado.org/ utes/utes_home.html.

Yelm, Betty, and Beals, Ralph. *Indians of the Park Region.* Rocky Mountain Nature Association, 1934.

The Tallest Mountain

"Expedition to the Yellow Stone." *Missouri Intelligencer*, March 25, 1820, p. 1. Accessed November 16, 2018. https://www.newspapers.com/image/338259532.

"Extract of a Letter from a Gentlemen Attached to the Yellow Stone Expedition, to His Friend in This Place, Dated Fort Missouri, Council Bluffs, Nov. 19." *Pittsburgh Weekly Gazette,* January 18, 1820. Accessed November 16, 2018. https://www.newspapers.com/image/96052672/?terms=Yellowstone%2BExpedition.

Fuller, Harlin M., and Hafen, LeRoy R., eds. The Journal of Captain John R. Bell, Official Journalist for the Stephen H. Long Expedition to the Rocky Mountains, 1820. Arthur H. Clark Company, Glendale, CA, 1957.

James, Edwin. Account of an Expedition from Pittsburgh to the Rocky Mountains, Performed in the Years 1819, 1820, by Order of the Hon. J. C. Calhoun, Secretary of War, Under the Command of Maj. S. H. Long, of the U.S. Top Engineers, Compiled from the Notes of Major Long, Mr. T. Say, and Other Gentlemen of the Party. Volume II. Longman, Hurst, Rees, Orme, and Brown, Paternoster-Row, London, 1823. Accessed November 15, 2018. https://play.google.com/books/reader?id=ys5jAAAAMAAJ&pg=GBS.PP9.

"Postscript." *The Bristol Mercury and Daily Post, Western Countries and South Wales Advertiser*, February 14, 1820, p. 2. Accessed November 16, 2018. https://www.newspapers.com/image/382722120/?terms=Yellowstone%2BExpedition.

The Summit Obtained

Hart, John L. J. "Seventy Years of Climbing on Longs Peak." *American Alpine Journal,* 1930. Accessed November 17, 2018. http://publications.americanalpineclub.org/articles/12193018200/Seventy-Years-of-Climbing-on-Longs-Peak.

Keplinger, Bruce. "Guide to the Keplinger Family Collection. University of Kansas Libraries." Kenneth Spencer Research Library, University of Kansas. Accessed November 18, 2018. http://etext.ku.edu/view?docId=ksrlead/ksrl.kc.keplinger bruce.xml;route=ksrlead;brand=ksrlead;query=.

Keplinger, L. W. "The First Ascent of Long's Peak, Made by an Expedition under Maj. J. W. Powell." *Collections of the Kansas State Historical Society 1915–1918*, ed. William E. Connelley. Vol. XIV. Kansas State Printing Plant, Topeka, 1918, pp. 340–353.

Lago, Don. "Jack Sumner Looks Back." Grand Canyon River Guides. Accessed November 18, 2018. https://www.gcrg.org/bqr/15-2/sumner.html.

MacDonald, Douglas. *Longs Peak: The Story of Colorado's Favorite Fourteener.* Westcliffe, Englewood, CO, 2004.

Toll, Oliver. *Arapaho Names & Trails.* Op. cit., pp. 40–41.

"The West Peak Climbers." *Denver Rocky Mountain News,* July 11, 1865, p. 1. Accessed November 17, 2018. https://newspaperarchive.com/denver-rocky-mountain-news-jul-11-1865-p-1.

Worster, Donald. *A River Running West: The Life of John Wesley Powell*. Oxford University Press, New York, 2001.

Summits in Skirts: The First Woman Climbers

"Anna Dickinson." *Rocky Mountain News*, August 9, 1873.

Bird, Isabella L. *A Lady's Life in the Rocky Mountains*. John Murray, London, 1879; University of Oklahoma Press, Norman, 1960.

Buchholtz, C. W. *Rocky Mountain National Park: A History*. Colorado Associated University Press, Boulder, 1983. Accessed November 18, 2018. https://www.nps.gov/parkhistory/online_books/romo/buchholtz/chap3.htm.

Byers, William (presumed). "The Hayden Expedition: From Middle Boulder to Long's Peak. The Country Passed Over—Ascent of Mount Long—The Trail—What Is Seen from the Summit." *Rocky Mountain News*, September 21, 1873. Accessed November 18, 2018. https://newspaperarchive.com/denver-rocky-mountain-news-sep-21-1873-p-2.

Dickinson, Anna Elizabeth. *A Ragged Register of People, Places and Opinions*. Harper & Brothers, New York, 1879.

Mills, Enos Abijah. *The Story of Estes Park and a Guide Book*. Outdoor Life, Estes Park, CO, 1905. Accessed December 13, 2018. https://books.google.com/books?id=h05OAAAAYAAJ&pg=PA18&lpg=PA18&dq=We+were+not+at+all+partial+to+such+an+arrangement+as+we+were+traveling+light+and+free&source=bl&ots=phQq5ktk8r&sig=M065sBrpP3tDgDyzgW0YoS53_zU&hl=en&sa=X&ved=2ahUKEwjio5TB6J3fAhUR0IMKHUCaBLwQ6AEwEXoECAgQAQ#v=onepage&q=We%20were%20not%20at%20all%20partial%20to%20such%20an%20arrangement%20as%20we%20were%20traveling%20light%20and%20free&f=false.

Robertson, Janet. *The Magnificent Mountain Women: Adventures in the Colorado Rockies*. University of Nebraska Press, Lincoln and London, 1990, 2003.

"A Trip in the Mountains and Up Long's Peak." *Greeley Sun*, August 14, 1873.

"A Woman on Longs Peak." *Boulder County News*, August 26, 1871.

Tragedy on the East Face: The Death of Agnes Vaille

Evans, Joseph R. *Death, Despair, and Second Chances in Rocky Mountain National Park*. Johnson Books, Boulder, CO, 2010. pp. 165–169.

"Girl Victim of Blizzard." *Nebraska State Journal*, January 14, 1925, p. 2. Accessed December 9, 2018. https://www.newspapers.com/image/314077592/?terms=Agnes%2BVaille.

"Kiener, Walter, 1894–1959." SNAC. Accessed December 9, 2018. http://snaccooperative.org/ark:/99166/w6wd8nwk.

Robertson, Janet. *The Magnificent Mountain Women*. Op. cit., pp. 47–56.

Sherman, John Dickinson. "Kiener's Lookout." *The Waterville Telegraph*, September 11, 1925, p. 7. Accessed December 9, 2018. https://www.newspapers.com/image/424465672/?terms=Agnes%2BVaille.

Sunnysummit. "Kiener's Route." SummitPost. Accessed December 9, 2018. https:// www.summitpost.org/kiener-s-route/155570.

Taylor, Carol, and Pettem, Silvia. "A Fatal Winter Climb in 1925." *Daily Camera*, January 11, 2013. Accessed December 9, 2018. http://www.dailycamera.com/ ci_22355341/agnes-vailles-longs-peak-fatal-winter-climb-1925.

The Quest for Gold and Silver

"Around the City." *Fort Collins Courier*, May 4, 1882, p. 3. Accessed November 26, 2018. https://newspaperarchive.com/fort-collins-courier-may-04-1882-p-3.

"'Bob' Womack May Recover." *The Weekly Gazette*, July 28, 1904, p. 1. Accessed November 27, 2018. https://www.newspapers.com/image/55942361/?terms=Robert %2BWomack.

Buchholtz, C. W. *Rocky Mountain National Park: A History*. Op. cit. Accessed November 28, 2018. https://www.nps.gov/parkhistory/online_books/romo/buchholtz/chap2 .htm.

Butler, William B. *Mining in Rocky Mountain National Park*. National Park Service, US Department of the Interior, 2006.

H. C. "Light for Lulu." *Fort Collins Courier*, September 9, 1880, p. 1. Accessed November 26, 2018. https://newspaperarchive.com/fort-collins-courier-sep-09 -1880-p-1.

H. C. "Lucky Lulu." *Fort Collins Courier*, August 26, 1880. Accessed November 26, 2018. https://newspaperarchive.com/fort-collins-courier-aug-26-1880-p-3.

Cairns, Mary Lyons. *Grand Lake: The Pioneers*. Renaissance House Publishers, Frederick, CO, 1946, 1991.

"Colorado Gold Rush." Colorado Encyclopedia. Accessed November 26, 2018. https:// coloradoencyclopedia.org/article/colorado-gold-rush.

"The Colorado Gold Rush." Western Mining History. Accessed November 26, 2018. https://westernmininghistory.com/articles/11/page1.

"For Pike's Peak . . ." *Chicago Tribune*, April 18, 1860, p. 1. Accessed November 26, 2018. https://www.newspapers.com/image/466103736/?terms=Pikes%2B Peak%2BGold%2BRush.

Garbella, E. J. "Gold Placer Mining in Colorado." *The Military Engineer*, Vol. XXIV, No. 138, 1932, p. 558. Accessed November 26, 2018. https://www.jstor.org/ stable/44566436?seq=1#page_scan_tab_contents.

"Ghost Town Whose History Is Unknown." *Craig Empire-Courier*, November 2, 1938, p. 6. Accessed November 26, 2018. https://newspaperarchive.com/craig-empire -courier-nov-02-1938-p-6.

"Grand Lake." *Fort Collins Courier*, August 6, 1885, p. 8. Accessed November 26, 2018. https://newspaperarchive.com/fort-collins-courier-aug-06-1885-p-8.

"HO for Lulu City." *Fort Collins Courier*, August 8, 1880. Accessed November 26, 2018. https://newspaperarchive.com/fort-collins-courier-aug-06-1880-p-3.

"The Isabella Gold Mine: Richest Strike in Mining History the World Has Ever Known." *Saranac Lake Adirondack News*, March 4, 1899, p. 2. Accessed November

27, 2018. https://newspaperarchive.com/saranac-lake-adirondack-news-mar-04 -1899-p-2.

"Lead Mountain Lodes—The Fourth at Lulu City." *Fort Collins Courier*, July 3, 1880, p. 2. Accessed November 26, 2018. https://newspaperarchive.com/fort-collins -courier-jul-08-1880-p-2.

"Longs Peak." *Longmont Ledger*, August 19, 1898, p. 2. Accessed November 27, 2018. https://newspaperarchive.com/longmont-ledger-aug-19-1898-p-2.

"Lulu City." *Denver Republican*, reprinted in the *Fort Collins Courier*, January 13, 1881. Accessed November 26, 2018. https://newspaperarchive.com/fort-collins-courier -jan-13-1881-p-4.

Mills, Enos. "Cripple Creek Nuggets." Paper copy of unpublished manuscript, Enos A. Mills Papers, Denver Public Library, 1897.

"Miners' Store." *Fort Collins Courier*, August 19, 1880. Accessed November 26, 2018. https://newspaperarchive.com/fort-collins-courier-aug-19-1880-p-3.

"Mining Notes." *Fort Collins Courier*, July 22, 1880, p. 3. Accessed November 26, 2018. https://newspaperarchive.com/fort-collins-courier-jul-22-1880-p-3.

"Off for Pike's Peak." *Chicago Tribune*, March 20, 1860, p. 1. Accessed November 26, 2018. https://www.newspapers.com/image/466103009/?terms=Pikes%2B Peak%2BGold%2BRush.

Richardson, A. D. "The Pike's Peak Gold Region." *Milwaukee Daily Sentinel*, March 29, 1860. Accessed November 21, 2018. https://newspaperarchive.com/milwaukee -daily-sentinel-mar-29-1860-p-2.

Spude, Robert L. "Allenspark Mining History Context 1859–1915: A Component of the Cultural Resource Assessment of Mining Sites within Rocky Mountain National Park." Paper copy of unpublished manuscript, Rocky Mountain Region Cultural Resources Division, Denver, 1990.

Troyer, Michael. "Treaty of Fort Wise." Colorado Encyclopedia. Last modified December 28, 2017. Accessed November 26, 2018. http://coloradoencyclopedia.org/ article/treaty-fort-wise.

Twitty, Eric. *Riches to Rust: A Guide to Mining in the Old West*. Western Reflections Publishing, Montrose, CO, 2002.

Frontier Hospitality

Atkins, D. Ferrel. "Earl of Dunraven." Rocky Mountain National Park, March 31, 2012. Accessed November 28, 2018. https://www.nps.gov/romo/earl_of_dunraven.htm.

"Colorado Briefs." *Elizabeth Elbert County Banner*, April 10, 1903, p. 2. Accessed November 28, 2018. https://newspaperarchive.com/elizabeth-elbert-county -banner-apr-10-1903-p-2.

"Colorado Items." *Alma Park County Bulletin*, October 20, 1905, p. 2. Accessed November 28, 2018. https://newspaperarchive.com/alma-park-county-bulletin-oct-20 -1905-p-2.

"The Estes Park Land Grab." *Fort Collins Standard*, August 26, 1874, p. 3. Accessed November 28, 2018. https://newspaperarchive.com/fort-collins-standard-aug-26 -1874-p-3.

Freudenburg, Betty D. *Facing the Frontier: The Story of the MacGregor Ranch*. Rocky Mountain Nature Association, Estes Park, CO, 1998, 2005.

"Lord Dunraven Surrenders Estes Park to Denver Capitalists." *Denver Post*, located in *Longmont Ledger*, April 21, 1905, p. 4. Accessed November 28, 2018. https://newspaperarchive.com/longmont-ledger-apr-21-1905-p-4.

Mote, James D. Historic Structure Report and Historic Furnishing Study, Holzwarth Homestead, Rocky Mountain National Park. National Park Service, US Department of the Interior, 1986.

"A New Company. . . ." *Greeley Tribune*, August 5, 1874, p. 2. Accessed November 28, 2018. https://newspaperarchive.com/greeley-tribune-aug-05-1874-p-2.

Nugent, James. "We are informed. . . ." *Fort Collins Standard*, August 12, 1874. Accessed November 28, 2018. https://newspaperarchive.com/fort-collins-standard-aug-12-1874-p-3.

Sprague, Abner. *My Pioneer Life: The Memoirs of an Estes Park Frontiersman*. Rocky Mountain Conservancy, Estes Park, CO, 2005, 2016.

Weiser-Alexander, Kathy. "Earl Dunraven and the Estes Park Land Grab." Legends of America. Accessed November 28, 2018. https://www.legendsofamerica.com/earl-dunraven-estes-park.

Wyndham-Quin, Windham Thomas, Earl of Dunraven. *Past Times and Pastimes*. Hodder and Stoughton, London, 1922. https://babel.hathitrust.org/cgi/pt?id=coo1.ark:/13960/t79s2bp9n;view=1up;seq=154.

The Killing of Mountain Jim

"A Correspondent of the *Tribune* recently took occasion. . . ." *Fort Collins Standard*, August 26, 1874, p. 3. Accessed December 4, 2018. https://newspaperarchive.com/fort-collins-standard-aug-26-1874-p-3. "Death of Mountain Jim." *Fort Collins Standard*, September 9, 1874, p. 3. Accessed December 4, 2018. https://newspaperarchive.com/fort-collins-standard-sep-09-1874-p-3.

"Griffith J. Evans was held to bail. . . ." *Fort Collins Standard*, July 22, 1874, p. 3. Accessed December 4, 2018. https://newspaperarchive.com/fort-collins-standard-jul-22-1874-p-3.

"The Mountain Jim Affair." *Fort Collins Standard*, September 2, 1874, p. 3. Accessed December 4, 2018. https://newspaperarchive.com/fort-collins-standard-sep-02-1874-p-3.

"Probate Court." *Fort Collins Standard*, October 14, 1874, p. 3. Accessed December 4, 2018. https://newspaperarchive.com/fort-collins-standard-oct-14-1874-p-3.

"Rocky Mountain Jim's Story." *Fort Collins Standard*, August 12, 1874, p. 3. Accessed December 4, 2018. https://newspaperarchive.com/fort-collins-standard-aug-12-1874-p-3.

Watrous, Ansel. "An Early Day Tragedy in Estes Park." *Estes Park Trail*, June 2, 1922. Accessed November 30, 2018. https://www.coloradohistoricnewspapers.org/cgi-bin/colorado?a=d&d=ETG19220602&e=-------en-20--1--txt-txIN--------0-.

Forever Preserved: Enos Mills and the Creation of a National Park

"Act to Establish a National Park Service (Organic Act), 1916." America's National Park System: The Critical Documents, National Park Service. Accessed December 1, 2018. https://www.nps.gov/parkhistory/online_books/anps/anps_1i.htm.

"The Antiquities Act of 1906, 16 USC 431-433." National Park Service Legislative and Congressional Affairs. Accessed December 1, 2018. https://www.nps.gov/subjects/legal/the-antiquities-act-of-1906.htm.

Buchholtz, C. W. "For the Benefit and Enjoyment of the People." *Rocky Mountain National Park: A History*. University Press of Colorado, Boulder, 1997. Accessed December 3, 2018. https://www.nps.gov/parkhistory/online_books/romo/buchholtz/chap5.htm.

"Dimensions of Estes National Park." *Longmont Ledger*, January 14, 1910, p. 1. Accessed December 3, 2018. https://newspaperarchive.com/longmont-ledger-jan-14-1910-p-1.

"Estes Park Plan Endorsed." *Lincoln Daily Star*, Nebraska, December 25, 1910, p. 16. Accessed December 3, 2018. https://newspaperarchive.com/lincoln-daily-star-dec-25-1910-p-16.

Fazio, Patricia M. "Cragged Crusade: The Fight for Rocky Mountain National Park 1909–1915." Master's thesis, Department of Recreation and Park Administration, Graduate School of the University of Wyoming, Laramie, 1982.

"From Enos A. Mills." *Longmont Ledger*, February 4, 1910, p. 4. Accessed December 3, 2018. https://newspaperarchive.com/longmont-ledger-feb-04-1910-p-4.

"Grow Trees Is His Advice." *Worth County Index*, March 21, 1907, p. 7. Accessed December 3, 2018. https://newspaperarchive.com/worth-county-index-mar-21-1907-p-7.

"Impetus to Park Movement." *Greeley Weekly Tribune*, September 14, 1911, p. 6. Accessed December 3, 2018. https://newspaperarchive.com/greeley-tribune-sep-14-1911-p-6.

Marshall, R. B. "Report on an Examination of the Area of the Proposed Rocky Mountain (Estes) National Park, Colorado." Records of the Office of the Secretary of the Interior, R. G. 79, National Archives, p. 11, January 9, 1913.

Mills, Enos A. "California: Seeing America First." Enos Mills Collection, 1914, box 1, file folder 18, Western History Department, Denver Public Library.

Mills, Enos A. "Rocky Mountain Forests." *Wild Life on the Rockies*, Houghton Mifflin, Riverside Press, Cambridge, Boston, and New York, 1909.

Mills, Enos A. *Your National Parks*. Houghton Mifflin, New York, 1917.

Mills, Enos A. *The Rocky Mountain National Park*. Doubleday, Page & Co., New York, 1924.

Mills, Enos A. "Going to the Top." *Enos Mills' Colorado*, ed. James H. Pickering. Johnson Books, Denver, 2006, 2018.

"The Proposed Estes National Park." *Longmont Ledger*, November 25, 1910, p. 4. Accessed December 3, 2018. https://newspaperarchive.com/longmont-ledger-nov-25-1910-p-4.

"A Snow Man: State Inspector Enos A. Mills Visits Greeley." *The Greeley Tribune*, March 23, 1905, p. 1. Accessed December 3, 2018. https://newspaperarchive.com/greeley-tribune-mar-23-1905-p-1.

The Birth of the Dude Ranch

Cairns, Mary Lyons. *Grand Lake: The Pioneers*. Renaissance House, Frederick, CO, 1946, reprinted as *Grand Lake in the Olden Days*, 1991.

Johnson, Richard S. "Living the Life of a Dude." *Empire Magazine*, December 1, 1974, pp. 66–72.

"Legacy of a Mountain Life." Rocky Mountain National Park. Accessed December 6, 2018. https://www.nps.gov/romo/planyourvisit/holzwarth-historic-site.htm.

Mote, James D. Historic Structure Report and Historic Furnishing Study, Holzwarth Homestead, Rocky Mountain National Park, Colorado. Op. cit.

The Highest Road

Albright, Horace. Report of the Director of the National Park Service to the Secretary of the Interior for the Fiscal Year Ended June 30, 1930. Government Printing Office, Washington, 1930, pp. 5, 30, 141. Accessed December 10, 2018. https://babel.hathitrust.org/cgi/pt?id=uc1.c021000380;view=1up;seq=11.

Bessemer, Louise. "New Terminals for Trail Ridge Road Being Advocated." *Greeley Tribune-Republican*, September 22, 1932, p. 11. Accessed December 11, 2018. https://newspaperarchive.com/greeley-daily-tribune-sep-22-1932-p-11.

Harrington, Daniel C. "The Trail Ridge Saga." Unpublished transcript on paper of an address delivered at Rocky Mountain National Park, July 17, 1982.

Learned, Clyde E. *Report on Fall River, West Side Section C (Final Construction)*. Bureau of Public Roads, September 27, 1932.

Mather, Stephen. *Report of the Director of the National Park Service to the Secretary of the Interior for the Fiscal Year Ended June 30, 1919*. Government Printing Office, Washington, 1919, pp. 22–27. Accessed December 10, 2018. https://babel.hathitrust.org/cgi/pt?id=mdp.39015006870839;view=1up;seq=7.

McClelland, Linda Flint. *Presenting Nature: The Historic Landscape Design of the National Park Service 1916 to 1942*. 1993. Accessed December 10, 2018. https://archive.org/details/present1916194200mccl/page/102.

Quillen, Robert. "Two Prices for State's Scenic Commercialization." *Greeley Tribune-Republican*, November 20, 1929, p. 10. Accessed December 11, 2018. https://newspaperarchive.com/greeley-daily-tribune-nov-20-1929-p-10.

Quinn, Richard. "Trail Ridge Road, Rocky Mountain National Park Between Estes Park and Grand Lake. . . ." *Historical American Engineering Record* HAER CO-31, National Park Service, US Department of the Interior, Washington, DC, 1993.

"Trail Ridge Highway Will Open in 1932." *Greeley Tribune-Republican*, October 17, 1931, p. 6. Accessed December 11, 2018. https://newspaperarchive.com/greeley-daily-tribune-oct-17-1931-p-6.

"Trail Ridge Road Will Be Finished Soon." *Greeley Tribune-Republican*, April 20, 1931, p. 13. Accessed December 11, 2018. https://newspaperarchive.com/greeley-daily-tribune-apr-20-1931-p-13.Wallace, S. A., Chief of Survey. "Report of Surveys, Rocky Mountain National Park, Colorado." US Department of Agriculture, Bureau of Public Roads, Denver, 1928.

"We Can Take It!" The Civilian Conservation Corps in Rocky Mountain

"Annual Report, 1937." Colorado State Department of Public Welfare, p. 39. Quoted in Brock, Julia, op. cit.

Brock, Julia. *A History of the CCC in Rocky Mountain National Park*. Rocky Mountain Nature Association and Rocky Mountain National Park, 2005. Accessed October 30, 2018. https://www.nps.gov/parkhistory/online_books/rmnp/ccc.pdf.

Chalana, Manish. "Colorado Cultural Resources Survey Form: Moraine Park Museum Amphitheater." UW Faculty, 2003. Accessed October 30, 2018. http://faculty.washington.edu/chalana/chalana%20moraine%20park%20report.pdf.

"Fishing." Rocky Mountain National Park. Accessed November 1, 2018. https://www.nps.gov/romo/planyourvisit/fishing.htm.

Gleyre, L. A., and Alleger, C. N. History of the Civilian Conservation Corps in Colorado, Littleton District—Grand Junction District. Press of the Western Newspaper Union, Denver, 1936.

(No author.) History of the Civilian Conservation Corps Colorado and Wyoming District. O'Brien Printing, Pueblo, CO, 1938.

"Moraine Lodge." *Estes Park Trail*, August 6, 1920. Accessed October 30, 2018. https://newspaperarchive.com/tags/?pep=moraine-lodge&pr=10&ob=1&page=4&pc=9217&psi=20&pci=7&pt=26233.

"Moraine Lodge." *Estes Park Trail*, September 2, 1921. Accessed October 30, 2018. https://newspaperarchive.com/tags/?pep=moraine-lodge&pr=10&ob=1&page=5&pc=9217&psi=20&pci=7&pt=26233.

"Moraine Lodge Dedicates Fine Rustic Assembly Hall." *Estes Park Trail*, July 27, 1923. Accessed October 30, 2018. https://newspaperarchive.com/estes-park-trail-talk-jul-27-1923-p-5.

"Moraine Park Museum and Amphitheater, Rocky Mountain National Park." National Park Service. Accessed October 30, 2018. https://www.nps.gov/articles/975211.htm#4/34.45/-98.53.

"Town and Countryside." *Estes Park Trail*, October 28, 1921. Accessed October 30, 2018. https://newspaperarchive.com/estes-park-trail-talk-oct-28-1921-p-4.

Yost, C. "National Register of Historic Places Registration Form." US Department of the Interior, National Park Service, March 14, 2005. Accessed October 30, 2018. http://legacy.historycolorado.org/sites/default/files/files/OAHP/NRSR/5LR477.pdf.

Yost, C., and Mardorf, C. "National Park Service Cultural Landscapes Inventory 2010: Moraine Park Museum and Amphitheater, Rocky Mountain National Park." National Park Service Integrated Resource Management Applications, 2010. Accessed October 30, 2018. https://irma.nps.gov/DataStore/DownloadFile/451386.

Returning to Nature

Allaback, Sarah. "Administration Building (Headquarters; Beaver Meadow Visitor Center), Rocky Mountain National Park, Estes Park, Colorado." *Mission 66 Visitor Centers: The History of a Building Type*. National Park Service. Accessed December 7, 2018. https://www.nps.gov/parkhistory/online_books/allaback/vc5.htm.

Boyer Buck, Barb. "On a mission to change RMNP." *Estes Park Trail Gazette*, April 10, 2015. Accessed December 7, 2018. http://www.eptrail.com/rocky-mountain -national-park/ci_27880726/mission-change-rmnp.

Butler, William B. *Mining in Rocky Mountain National Park*. Rocky Mountain National Park, National Park Service, US Dept. of the Interior, 2006.

Bzdek, Maren Thompson, and Ore, Janet. "The Mission 66 Program at Rocky Mountain National Park: 1947–1973." Colorado State University Public Lands History Center, 2010. Accessed December 7, 2018. https://publiclands.colostate.edu/wp -content/uploads/sites/57/2013/12/mission66.pdf.

Habecker, Shawn L. "Abandoned Structures in the Landscape: Off Campus Field Study Proposal." Student paper, Rocky Mountain National Park curator's files, April 28, 1994.

"The History of Estes Park Lodge #183 AF and AM." Estes Park Masonic Lodge. Accessed December 8, 2018. http://www.estesparkmasoniclodge.com/about.

Jessen, Kenneth. "Bear Lake—Once an Unsightly Mess." *Loveland Reporter-Herald*, January 3, 2015. Accessed December 8, 2018. "National Parks' Homefront Battle: Protecting Parks During WWII." National Park Service. Accessed December 7, 2018. https://www.nps.gov/articles/npshomefrontbattle.htm.

Jessen, Kenneth. "Hidden Valley Ski Area at Rocky Mountain National Park Lasted Nearly 60 Years." *Loveland Reporter-Herald*, February 7, 2015. Accessed December 7, 2018. http://www.reporterherald.com/columnists/colorado-history/ci _27471491/hidden-valley-ski-area-at-rocky-mountain-national.

"New Park Visitor Center Will Be Located Near Present NPS Utility Area." *Estes Park Trail*, September 4, 1964, p. 1.

"Rocky Mountain National Park." NPS Stats: National Park Service Visitor Use Statistics. Accessed December 7, 2018. https://irma.nps.gov/Stats/SSRSReports/ Park%20Specific%20Reports/Annual%20Park%20Recreation%20Visitation%20 (1904%20-%20Last%20Calendar%20Year)?Park=ROMO.

INDEX

ABOUT THE AUTHOR

Best-selling author **Randi Minetor** has written more than forty books for Rowman & Littlefield, including *Historic Glacier National Park* and five books that tell the true stories of people who have died in national and state parks: *Death on Mount Washington, Death on Katahdin, Death in Acadia National Park, Death in Glacier National Park,* and *Death in Zion National Park.* Her work extends to birding guides, including *Backyard Birding, Birding New England,* and *The New England Bird Lover's Garden,* as well as guides to a number of national parks and historic cities and eight books on the best day hikes in New York State. Randi writes for a number of trade magazines in theater technology, medicine, municipal water management, and tourism, and she serves as a ghostwriter for executives and entrepreneurs in a wide range of fields. She is based in Rochester, New York.